Wow. Charles Spurgeon wro
Apocalypse by the famed S
Harman, who has written ext
its message for us today. Y
anywhere else.   Pastor Jimmy Reagan – Leesville, SC
            Author of *Obadiah: Showing the Path of Peace*

I have known Jim for many years and I have always admired his wisdom, virtue, and his passion for the Lord. In *Daniel's Prophecies Unsealed*, Jim has proven once again that he is willing to challenge even his own traditions to uphold his integrity and, even more importantly, the integrity of God's Word. For the open minded scholar, this book will provoke you to carefully read and re-read the well organized details and arguments that Jim puts forth. For all readers, you will be encouraged to anticipate and prepare for the return of our Lord Jesus Christ!   Pastor Jeff Philips – Orlando, FL

With his newest book, *Daniel's Prophecy Unsealed*, I am once again amazed by Jim Harman's diligent research into Bible prophecy and by his thorough presentation of End-time truth.
            Pastor Mike Dawson – Columbia, TN

Daniel's Prophecies Unsealed is a wonderful blend of scholarship with an open heart to the Lord. It is extremely helpful in understanding the book of Daniel. Whether you are a new Bible student or scholar, I highly recommend it.
            Pastor Steve Snyder – Clearlake, CA

Daniel's Prophecies Unsealed is a well researched, clear presentation that focuses on deciphering the hidden message that has been needed for a very long time. The author cuts through the confusion in an elegant manner to show how close we are to the end-times. This timely book not only begs the question "Just how close are we," but also makes the reader question: are you prepared – mentally, spiritually, fiscally?
            John Zajac – San Jose, CA
            Author of *The Delicate Balance*

In these times characterized by the proliferation of false teachings and personal egocentric preaching of the Word of God, it is refreshing to find a man of integrity with a passion for the truth and God given gifts in the person of Jim Harman. I encourage all those seeking to receive light relevant to the days we live, to read *Daniel's Prophecies Unsealed*. As you read the well presented information it contains, pray for the Holy Spirit to guide you and let God impel you to reach others for his kingdom, as that day draws near. Thank you Jim for letting God use you in helping reveal the pieces of the puzzle.

Pastor Justino Rolon – Orlando, FL

Any book that challenges the traditional false teachings, including that the USA cannot be found in the Scriptures needs to be read by all. *Daniel's Prophecies Unsealed* does exactly that and more. It challenges all of us to stay in the word of God as these events are rapidly coming to a grand and final conclusion. May God grant us the wisdom to become and stay wise and not foolish.   Lyndon Navarre – Port St. Lucie, FL

I encourage all students of God's Word to read James Harman's new book *Daniel's Prophecies Unsealed*. It provides an in-depth understanding of the five visions given to Daniel, which were given to those who love and eagerly look forward to the soon return of Jesus Christ.   Charles Strong – Harlingen, TX
Bible One Ministry (www.bibleone.net)

I am so very grateful for Jim Harman's books since the 1990's, including his new writing on Daniel. No question about it – he was raised up by God for those Christians in the last days that hunger and thirst for God's righteousness after we've been born into God's family.   Joan Olsen – Yukon, OK

Daniel's Prophecies
Unsealed

Understanding the Time of the End

James T. Harman

**Prophecy
Countdown
Publications**

Daniel's Prophecies Unsealed

Prophecy Countdown Publications, LLC
P.O. Box 941612
Maitland, FL 32794
www.ProphecyCountdown.com
ISBN: 978-0-9636984-9-0

All references from Scripture are from the New King James Version unless noted otherwise:

AMP	Amplified Bible, copyright ©1987 Lockman Foundation
ESV	English Standard Version®, copyright ©2001 Crossway
KJ	King James Version, copyright ©1982
NAS	New American Standard Bible, copyright ©1960
NIV	New International Version, copyright ©1973
NLT	New Living Translation, copyright ©1996
YLT	Young's Literal Translation, copyright ©1898

Scripture abbreviations as used throughout this book are from the Blue Letter Bible (www.BlueLetterBible.org), and they are summarized on p. 79. Numerical references to selected words in the text of Scripture are from James H. Strong Dictionaries of the Hebrew and Greek words.

Words in bold emphasis are author's and not in original Scripture. Certain words such as Kingdom and Judgment Seat of Christ are capitalized to emphasize their importance, but not in accordance with traditional fashions. Certain numerical values are used for clarity or emphasis in presentation and not in accordance with guidelines recommended by all traditional practices.

Cover image of UN and statue by Steve Creitz, www.ProphecyArt.com
Back cover image of flags at UN by M. Bergsma, www.Travel-Images.com

---

NOTE TO READER

The purpose of this writing is not to provide a verse-by-verse commentary of the entire book of Daniel. Many other authors have provided such works. The main objective of this book is to focus on helping the reader discover the wonderful message God has for us as we approach the final days and the prophecies are being unsealed.

Throughout this book, bibliographical references may be provided in the comments on selected texts with the commentator's last name along with page numbers (in parenthesis) for the references cited.

Prologue

The prophecies in the book of Daniel are some of the most difficult passages in the Bible, causing many to avoid studying this valuable book. To complicate matters, many liberal interpreters don't even believe Daniel wrote it! They try to prove it was written after the prophecies were fulfilled, thereby challenging its Divine inspiration. This short work will not take the time to address this essential issue since it has been refuted quite admirably by many highly regarded scholars.[1]

Unlike the book of Revelation, which is not sealed, Daniel was told to seal up the words in the book until the time of the end. I have been striving to understand Daniel's prophecies for over three decades; but understanding God's prophetic Word is progressive in nature as we get closer to the time of Christ's return and as Daniel's prophecies are being unsealed. I believe the time is very short and that God placed these prophecies in the Bible to make known His final plan.

Very significantly, Daniel was told that the wise would be able to understand the message while the wicked would not know what it means. When Jesus sat on the Mount of Olives just before His crucifixion, He similarly described two types of believers living in the last days. He told his disciples that some would be wise and some would be foolish and that some would be wise and faithful, while others would be wicked and slothful. Jesus told them that the wise and faithful would be richly rewarded (Mat 24:45-47; 25:23) while the wicked, foolish and slothful (Mat 24:48-51; 25:24-30) would be chastised at the time of the Lord's return.

Since Daniel was told that the wise will understand the message and lead many to righteousness, while the wicked will not grasp the meaning of the prophecies and will continue in their wickedness, it is imperative for everyone living in these latter days to diligently examine and attempt to comprehend the vital message Daniel has recorded for us.

Several years ago we learned that Sir Isaac Newton understood the Hebrew language and that he translated Daniel's prophecies. He felt that Daniel gave us a prophecy about both the **first** and **second** comings of Christ. While we do not know if Newton's interpretation is correct, we are including his findings, because if he is right, then the Lord's return may be imminent.

The primary focus of this study is to discover the meaning of some of the most amazing visions recorded in the Bible. Its purpose is not to set a date for end time events, nor are the speculations in this book meant to assert dogmatic identities of the various nations associated with the prophecies.

I believe that Daniel wrote this most important book and that God gave him five critical visions for those living in the end times. Some believe all of Daniel's prophecies have already been fulfilled; however, we feel that his message is for today!

Israel celebrated their 70th anniversary as a nation on May 14, 2018. Jesus told us the generation to witness their rebirth would not pass away (Mat 24:32-34). The question then becomes: how long is a generation? The Psalms tell us:

> *"The days of our lives are **seventy years** And if by reason of strength they are **eighty years**, Yet their boast is only labor and sorrow; For it is soon cut off, and we fly away...**So teach us to number our days**, That we may gain a **heart of wisdom**"* (Psa 90:10, 12 – KJ).

When Jesus came the first time, the wise men of the day were aware of His soon arrival since they were actively looking for Him. The prophet Daniel said at the time of the end *"the wise would understand."* May the Lord grant us a heart of wisdom to understand the time we are living in!

Dedication

For all those
who love His appearing

"... *there is laid up for me the* **crown of righteousness,**
which the Lord, the righteous Judge,
will give to me on that Day,
and not to me only but also
to all who have loved His appearing."
(2Ti 4:8)

"...*Looking for that blessed hope,*
and the glorious appearing
of the great God and
our Saviour Jesus Christ..."
(Titus 2:13 – KJ)

How Long is a Generation?

"Now learn a parable of the fig tree; When his branch is yet tender, and putteth forth leaves, ye know that summer is nigh: So likewise ye, when ye shall see all these things, know that it is near, even at the doors. Verily I say unto you, **This generation shall not pass, till all these things be fulfilled***"* (Matthew 24:32-36 – KJ).

What was the average life expectancy at the time of Jesus?

Those living in the days of **Jesus** (as mentioned in the New Testament) had an **average life span** that was similar to human life spans before the arrival of modern medicine and technology. At the time Jesus spoke the above words, the **average life expectancy** was around 30 to 35 years, similar to the **life span** of those in Classical Rome.

> 32 AD + 35 = 67 AD around the time that the Romans' siege of Jerusalem began (3½ years of tribulation), ending in 70 AD.

In 1948 the average life expectancy was approximately 70 years (or 80 because of strength as in Psalm 90).

> 1948 + 70 = 2018 +?

"The days of our life are **seventy years**— *Or even, if because of strength,* **eighty years***; Yet their pride [in additional years] is only labor and sorrow, For it is soon gone and we fly away"* (Psalm 90:10 – AMP).

Table of Contents

> *"11) Behold, the days are coming,"*
> *says the Lord GOD,*
> *That I will **send a famine on the land**,*
> *Not a famine of bread,*
> *Nor a thirst for water,*
> *But of **hearing the words of the LORD**.*
> *12) They shall wander from sea to sea,*
> *And from north to east;*
> *They shall run to and fro,*
> *seeking the word of the LORD,*
> *But shall not find it.*
> (Amo 8:11-12)

*"But you, Daniel, shut up the words, and seal the book until the time of the end; many shall run to and fro, and **knowledge shall increase**"* (Dan 12:4).

Daniel's visions were given for those living at the time of the end. The wise will diligently search the word of the Lord and ask for wisdom. These prophecies have been given to us so that we can understand God's plan during these final days before He comes to set up His new Kingdom.

None of the wicked will understand, but those who are wise will understand.

Foreword

It always amazes me to witness the signature of God in our daily lives. This has been the case with my friend and brother in the faith, James T. Harman. When our Creator sets His love upon someone and causes them to be born of the Spirit, *"he is a new creature, old things are passed away: behold all things are become new."* This has been true for James Harman. God tells us in Ephesians 2:10, *"For we are his workmanship, created in Christ Jesus unto good works, which God hath before ordained that we should walk in them."*

Before the foundation of the world, God had already established the *"good works"* that He had already prepared for Jim to fulfill. *Daniel's Prophecies Unsealed* is one of those good works God was referring to. Of course, James Harman had no idea regarding these amazing plans. God tells us why in Jeremiah 33:3, *"Call unto me and I will show you great and mighty things that thou knowest not."*

The prophet Daniel is the Apostle Paul of the Old Testament. God revealed to no one that amount of revelation that He did to Daniel. Daniel even had to tell his Creator to hold his hand, that his soul was not able to contain all that was being revealed to him.

And what makes it even more amazing is that our Lord Jesus has given James a very special task: to make known that which has been sealed for so long a time. As it is written in Daniel 12, where God instructed His servant that the words He was giving him were closed up, that they were to be sealed until the time of the end...when those who are wise will be able to understand. These endtime revelations of God's Word to His servant Daniel are rarely referenced by Bible teachers through the ages, for good reason. Though the words given to Daniel were like a time capsule, to be sealed for a long period of time and then to be unsealed in the endtimes. Though sealed, they were still true, to be unsealed at the appropriate time, and we have come to that time. Moreover, God has called James Harman to be one of those to provide the wise with understanding.

We are entering the final days of our Lord's return. The timing of the signless event of the rapture will also be known only to our Creator as it is not for us to know. God only required of us to watch and pray for the signs and the strength to continue faithful. We have all been witnessing things in the world that we never dreamed we would see, especially in our own country. Nothing should surprise us as the Bible warned us that there would be a hurricane of apostasy and that the nations would become more lawless as the end draws near. That hurricane season of apostasy may be upon us.

May our Lord Jesus be pleased to use this book in the life of every believer as He has graciously used it in causing our co-heir of God, James Harman, to write those words on paper.

Dr. John Barela, D.D., Ph.D.
Today, the Bible and You

Introduction

We are about to explore some of the most important prophecies recorded in the Word of God. While the book of Daniel contains a wealth of familiar stories and teachings that are well loved by most students of the Bible, the focus of this brief commentary will be on the five supernatural visions Daniel was given over 2,500 years ago.

God's original purpose was to make the descendants of Abraham the leading nation of the world; however, their disobedience and idolatry after King Solomon prevented this. Around 721–2 BC the northern "Ten Tribes" were led into captivity in Assyria, and in 605–6 BC the remaining two Tribes of Judah were taken by Nebuchadnezzar into Babylon.

As one of the captives, Daniel was taken from his homeland to reside in the foreign land of Babylon. He was a man of prayer and devout faith that was greatly tested living in such a pagan society. He led an exemplary life and because he would not compromise, God's hand was on this young man. The Lord honored Daniel's faithfulness and he was bestowed with divine knowledge and wisdom and was promoted to a leadership position in King Nebuchadnezzar's court. As a result of Daniel's life, we are the beneficiaries of five amazing visions that provide a preview of what's in store during these final days.

The book of Daniel can be divided into two parts: chapters 1-6, which are generally considered historical (except the vision in chapter 2); and chapters 7-12, which contain the remaining prophetical sections.

The **first vision** occurred when God revealed the mystery of King Nebuchadnezzar's famous dream of the great image depicted on the front cover (Daniel 2). This famous prophecy spans the entire time from Babylon's kingdom until God sets up

His Kingdom on the earth at the second coming of Christ. The meaning of the king's dream was given to Daniel in a night vision, and it reveals that all earthly kingdoms will come to an end when Jesus returns in the very near future.

The traditional interpretation of the **second vision** of the four great beasts of Daniel 7 asserts they are the same empires depicted by the four kingdoms in Nebuchadnezzar's dream. We believe these beasts represent four Gentile nations that have or will arise from the turn of the 20th century until the second coming of Christ. Readers are encouraged to see Appendix 1, before reading about the four great beasts, to understand how traditional interpretations can lead us astray.

The **third vision** Daniel received is of a ram, goat and a little horn in Daniel 8 and may be the most difficult one to decipher. Because the book of Revelation describes both the Antichrist and the false prophet, we believe God would not have omitted the false prophet in His revelation to Daniel, which we feel Daniel describes in this vision.

Daniel's **fourth vision** is one of the greatest prophecies recorded in the Word of God. The 70 Weeks of Daniel, found in Daniel 9, is misunderstood by most people living today. This is because the traditional teaching taught today is a relatively new invention. Readers are encouraged to approach this chapter with an open mind and a teachable heart; those who do will be amazed by this magnificent prophecy.

Daniel's **fifth vision** of the time of end covers the final three chapters: Daniel 10, 11 and 12. The prophecies given in these closing chapters are the most detailed examples of history written in advance that God revealed to Daniel.

*"Now I have come to make you understand what will happen to Your people **in the latter days**, for the vision refers to **Many days yet to come**"* (Dan 10:14).

It is important to understand that the term the *latter days* has a dual meaning. When this was given to Daniel, it referred to the **first coming** of Jesus Christ to announce the kingdom to the Jewish people. But because God foreknew Jesus would be rejected by the Jews, the *latter days* also represents the time before the **second coming** of Christ.

The latter days described in Daniel 11 provide a detailed history from about 300–175 BC. These are *literal* prophecies that historians have been able to trace. Certain parts of these prophecies will also have a *prophetic* fulfillment in the times just prior to Christ's second coming. The literal fulfillments serve as types or pictures of what will take place in the future prophetic fulfillments. Daniel's fifth vision has been partially fulfilled in the past, but it will also be fulfilled during the final days we are living in.

For students of the Bible, these are exciting times to be alive. The five visions given to Daniel are nearing their final fulfillment. While we don't know precisely when Jesus will come or how all of the various prophecies will be accomplished, we know that it is imperative to be prepared. Many who are not ready will be sorely tried and tested in the days ahead.

Now, more than ever, we need to remember the type of life that Daniel lived. He stood up for God's word and separated himself from the pagan world in which he lived. He lived a holy life remaining faithful and obedient to his calling. His life is a great object lesson for those of us living today. We live in a modern Babylon culture where our values are put on trial every day. May our lives be modeled by the example of this remarkable man who was "greatly beloved" by God.

"...when He is revealed, we shall be like Him, for we shall see Him as He is. ***And everyone who has this hope in Him purifies himself, just as He is pure"*** (1Jo 3:2-3 – ESV).

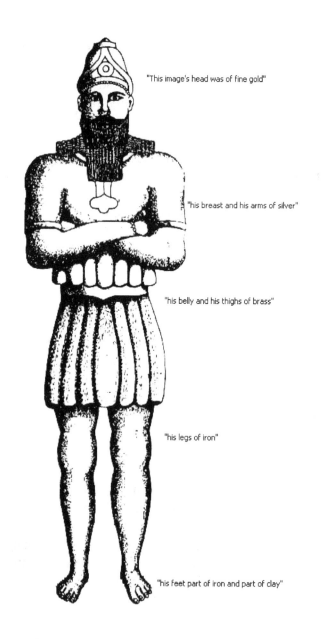

"This image's head was of fine gold"

"his breast and his arms of silver"

"his belly and his thighs of brass"

"his legs of iron"

"his feet part of iron and part of clay"

The above picture was adapted from *Dispensational Truth,* by Clarence Larkin, page 125, © 1918. Used with permission of the Rev. Clarence Larkin Estate, P.O. Box 334, Glenside, PA 19038, U.S.A., 215-576-5590, www.larkinestate.com

Chapter 1 – Vision of the Latter Days

King Nebuchadnezzar was given one of the most famous dreams recorded in the Bible. None of the king's wise men or magicians could interpret his dream, but Daniel told the king:

> *"...27) The secret which the king has demanded, the wise men, the astrologers, the magicians, and the soothsayers cannot declare to the king. 28) But there is a God in heaven who reveals secrets, and He has made known to King Nebuchadnezzar what will be in the latter days"* (Dan 2:27-28).

Daniel tells the king that the God of heaven gave the king a dream that concerns the *latter days*. As described in the introduction to this book, the term *latter days* refers to both the time before Christ's first advent and the time before His second coming. The king was given a dream that spans from the time of his kingdom until the time when Jesus returns.

King's Dream

> *"31) You, O king, were watching; and behold, a great image! This great image, whose splendor was excellent, stood before you; and its form was awesome. 32) This image's **head** was of fine gold, its **chest and arms** of silver, its **belly and thighs** of bronze, 33) its **legs** of iron, its **feet** partly of iron and partly of clay. 34) You watched while a **stone** was cut out without hands, which struck the image on its feet of iron and clay, and broke them in pieces. 35) Then the iron, the clay, the bronze, the silver, and the gold were crushed together, and became like chaff from the summer threshing floors; the wind carried them away so that no trace of them was found. And the stone that struck the image became a great mountain and filled the whole earth"* (Dan 2:31-35).

Daniel disclosed the details of the king's dream, which God had revealed to him. The great image of this statue has been the subject of much debate and contention over the years. The following is the interpretation that was given to Daniel:

Daniel's Interpretation

*"38)...you are this head of gold. 39) But after you shall arise another kingdom inferior to yours; then another, a third kingdom of bronze, which shall rule over all the earth. 40) And the fourth kingdom shall be as strong as iron, in as much as iron breaks in pieces and shatters everything; and like iron that crushes, that kingdom will break in pieces and crush all the others. 41) Whereas you saw the feet and toes, partly of potter's clay and partly of iron, the kingdom shall be divided; yet the strength of the iron shall be in it, just as you saw the iron mixed with ceramic clay. 42) And as the toes of the feet were partly of iron and partly of clay, so the kingdom shall be partly strong and partly fragile. 43) As you saw iron mixed with ceramic clay, they will mingle with the seed of men; but they will not adhere to one another, just as iron does not mix with clay. 44) And in the days of these kings the **God of heaven will set up a kingdom which shall never be destroyed**; and the kingdom shall not be left to other people; it shall break in pieces and consume all these kingdoms, and it shall stand forever. 45) In as much as you saw that the **stone was cut out of the mountain without hands**, and that it broke in pieces the iron, the bronze, the clay, the silver, and the gold—the great God has made known to the king what will come to pass after this. **The dream is certain, and its interpretation is sure**"* (Dan 2:38-45).

The above interpretation declares that all of the kingdoms of the statue will ultimately be destroyed by the stone[1] (Jesus) when He returns to set up the Kingdom of God.

It is important to realize that this dream reveals the gentile powers that would dominate Daniel's people. The statue begins with the _head of gold_, which represented King Nebuchadnezzar. The second inferior kingdom shown by the _chest and arms of silver_ was the Med-Persian empire, which arose in 539 BC (also depicted by the ram with two horns in Daniel 8:20). The third kingdom represented by the _belly and thighs of bronze_ was Greece that came under Alexander the Great in 331 BC. The fourth ruler over the Holy Land of Israel was the Roman Empire portrayed by the strong _legs of iron_. The Romans ruled over the people of Israel from 63 BC to 70 AD[2] when their temple was destroyed and the Jews were scattered from their land.

It is important to notice that Daniel's interpretation of the dream does not resume again until the time he discusses the **feet and toes**, "_partly of potter's clay and partly of iron, the kingdom shall be divided; yet the strength of the iron shall be in it, just as you saw the iron mixed with ceramic clay_" (Dan 2:41).

The feet and toes represent ten nations, which will arise at the _time of the end_. This is verified by other parts of Daniel (Dan 7:7) and Revelation (Rev 13:1). In other words, the details of the statue won't be fully understood until the time that these nations emerge on the world scene because the interpretation states: _And in the days of these kings_ the **God of heaven will set up a kingdom which shall never be destroyed** (Dan 2:44).

Students of Bible prophecy are well aware that the nation of Israel is one of the most vital keys to events during the latter days. Until the rebirth of Israel in 1948 and their recapture of the city of Jerusalem in 1967, Daniel's night vision of the king's dream had been put on hold. But now, with the restoration of their nation, the time for these ten nations to appear is here. Also remember that these prophecies have been sealed until the time of the end. The actual identity of these ten nations will be revealed as God unseals this prophecy.

Commentators are divided over whether these ten countries will be part of a revived Roman empire or if they represent ten Middle Eastern nations who will unite against the people of Israel. The following diagram helps outline the debate:

	Roman Antichrist? Babylon	Islamic Antichrist? Babylon
	Med-Persian Empire	Med-Persian Empire
	Grecian Empire	Grecian Empire
	Roman Empire	Moslem Empire (a)
	Ten Roman Nations	Ten Islamic Nations

(a) Some see the fourth kingdom as Alexander's successors with the Seleucid / Ptolemy kingdoms as the two legs.

Several of the Interpreters for the Fourth Kingdom

Roman		Moslem / Islamic
Josephus	Newton	Westcott
Barnabas	Pusey	Delitzsch
Irenaeus	Keil	Driver
Origen	Bullinger	Montgomery
Jerome	*Most modern*	Porphyry
Augustine	*dispensationalists*	Rosenmuller
Luther	*and evangelical*	Stuart
Calvin	*churches*	Zockler

The identity of the ten nations represented by the statue's feet partially hinges upon understanding the meaning of the following:

> "....41) *partly of potter's clay and partly of iron*, the kingdom shall be divided; yet the strength of the iron shall be in it, just as you saw the iron mixed with ceramic clay. 43) As you saw iron mixed with ceramic clay, they will **mingle** [arab] with the seed of men; but they will not adhere to one another, just as iron does not mix with clay" (Dan 2:41, 43).

Interpreters vary widely over the meaning of the above verses. Clearly, the iron and clay nations will not mix very well together. Some suggest the iron represents communist nations with dictatorships while the clay nations signify democracies.

A few commentators have noted that the word "mingle" in verse 43 was written in Aramaic and the root word means "arab." They suggest this could be a reference to the desire to unite their kingdoms by marriage, which was a characteristic of the Syrian and Egyptian kings who resorted to intermarriage.

Several have inferred that these verses may be related to the United Nations (UN). The current Security Council consists of 15 members: 5 permanent and 10 non-permanent member nations. The 5 permanent nations are: England, Russia, France, China and the United States. Interestingly, these five countries are a mixture of communist and democratic nations.

Over the years there has been a great deal of speculation that the UN was considering increasing the permanent membership to 10 countries. Whether the permanent number of seats will be increased is unknown, but it could be related to a possible fulfillment of Daniel's prophecies. More may become apparent with developments within the UN as time goes on.

Finally, a few interpreters believe the *"potter's clay"* is a reference to Jeremiah: *"O house of Israel, can I not do with you as this potter? Says the Lord. Look, as the clay is in the potter's hand, so are you in My hand"* (Jer 18:6). Could this be a reference to the Israeli tribes that migrated to Europe and America as some expositors suggest?

Or, as noted by commentator Stephen Miller: "...the peoples who made up ancient Rome and who will come together to form the final phase of that empire during the last days have continued to survive throughout the centuries through various nations and empires, particularly those of Europe. In that sense the Roman Empire has never ceased to exist" (Miller, p.99).

Daniel's interpretation of the mixture of iron and clay could be a cryptic reference to some form of European federation of ten nations who will eventually unite with the coming Antichrist during the last days.

As we will discover in the next chapter, Daniel's second vision of the four great beasts will provide additional enlightenment surrounding the nations that will come together during these final days. This will be corroboration that all of the kingdoms of the statue in King Nebuchadnezzar's dream will ultimately be destroyed by the stone (Jesus) when He returns to set up the Kingdom of God, precisely as Daniel's interpretation declared.

This exact same scenario is verified by the Apostle John:

> *"12) The ten horns which you saw are **ten kings who have received no kingdom as yet**, but they **receive authority for one hour as kings with the beast**. 13) These are of one mind, and they will give their power and authority to the beast. 14) **These will make war with the Lamb**, and the Lamb will overcome them, for He is Lord of lords and King of kings"* (Rev 17:12-14).

Chapter 2 – Vision of the Four Beasts

Some of the most important prophecies regarding the time of the end are described in Daniel 7. Unfortunately, the traditional interpretation has misconstrued the true meaning by asserting that the four kingdoms described in King Nebuchadnezzar's dream are the same as the four beasts in this chapter.

The image in Daniel 2 represents the four kingdoms of Babylon, Med-Persia, Greece and Rome, while the four great beasts in Daniel 7 symbolize four nations that will arise _at the time of the end_ just prior to the second coming of Christ. Most significantly, two of the four beasts have already emerged on the world scene and the two remaining beasts are about to make their grand entrance.

> _"1) In the first year of Belshazzar king of Babylon, Daniel had a **dream and visions** of his head while on his bed. Then he wrote down the dream, telling the main facts. 2) Daniel spoke, saying, 'I saw in my vision by night, and behold, the four winds of heaven were stirring up the Great Sea.' 3) And <u>four great beasts came up from the sea</u>, each different from the other."_ (Daniel 7:1-3)

In Scripture, the sea represents Gentile nations of the world, and the Great Sea most likely represents the area around the Mediterranean Sea. Daniel's vision pictures four great nations that arrive during tumultuous times among the nations. This clearly is a reference to the last century, which witnessed two world wars with devastation and loss of life unlike any other time in human history. The very first beast to come up from the sea is described as a lion with wings like an eagle that are plucked off and given the heart of a man.

*"4) The **first** was **like a lion**, and had eagle's wings. I watched till its wings were plucked off; and it was lifted up from the earth and made to stand on two feet like a man, and a man's heart was given to it"* (Dan 7:4).

The Lion is well recognized as a symbol for Great Britain. At the turn of the last century, Great Britain was a dominant force in the world with their mighty navy ruling the seas. They were greatly blessed by God, and their nation was instrumental in helping the Jewish people return to their homeland with the issuance of the Balfour Declaration in 1917.

Between 1917 and 1948, Great Britain became opposed to the Jews due to the political situation with the Arabs. The term **beast** represents a nation that is in opposition to the people of Israel. During this time Great Britain became the **beast** as described by Daniel, because of their antagonism toward Israel. As predicted, their "wings" (representing their great power) were "plucked off" and their political, economic and military power has been deeply diminished ever since.

After the Jews established the State of Israel in 1948, Great Britain ceased their opposition to the Jewish people. This is pictured by Daniel as the beast being given a *"man's heart,"* and they have been more favorable toward Israel ever since. This will likely change in the near future when Great Britain turns, once again, and joins forces as one of the *"ten horns"* (Dan 7:7) with the Antichrist.

Daniel then describes the second beast that rises out of the sea as a bear:

*"And suddenly another beast, a **second**, **like a bear**. It was raised up on one side, and had three ribs in its mouth between its teeth. And they said thus to it: 'Arise, devour much flesh!'"* (Dan 7:5)

The interpreters[1] who recognize that the four beasts in Daniel 7 are all in existence at the time of the second coming of Christ mainly agree that Great Britain is the lion. Most also recognize Russia as the second beast, described as a bear.

The "three ribs" in the bear's mouth stand for the time in 1940 when the Baltic countries of Lithuania, Estonia and Latvia were annexed by Russia. During the last World Wars, millions upon millions of people were slain and much blood was shed. No other country on earth is more aptly described as having "devoured much flesh."

Russia has always been in opposition to Israel, providing weapons, military leadership and training to many of the Arab nations who want to see Israel destroyed. The Russian bear is a most voracious and fierce predatory beast depicted as the second beast to rise up from the sea of nations.

It is important to realize that the first two beasts in Daniel's vision are already present on the world scene! These two countries are present and active participants in the world today. The third and fourth beasts are about to surface!

The identity of the third beast is a little more difficult to detect.

> *"After this I looked, and there was another, **like a leopard**, which had **on its back four wings of a bird**. The beast also had **four heads**, and **dominion was given to it**"* (Dan 7:6).

The third beast that is about to materialize is described as a leopard with four heads with four wings on its back. The dictionary[2] defines leopard as: *"**A lion in side view, having one forepaw raised and the head facing the observer.**"* This definition of a leopard provides us a perfect picture of a **sphinx**, which happens to be one of the international symbols for Egypt.

While a few expositors envision Germany as the third beast, Egypt is a better match to what the Scripture actually portrays. To decipher the meaning of Daniel's four beasts it is important to remember that these great nations will come from "*the four winds of heaven...stirring of the Great Sea*" (Dan 7:3).

The countries are shown arriving on the scene shaping events associated with the land of Israel during the time of the end. The lion (Great Britain) came from the *west* of the sea, the bear (Russia) is located *north* and *east* of the sea, and the third beast pictured as a leopard should be expected to come from the *south* of the sea. Besides location, Egypt is the most likely candidate to fulfill the prophetic role of Daniel's leopard for several reasons.

The leopard is pictured with four wings like a bird. The map below shows how four nations appear to be attached to the back of Egypt at the Sinai Peninsula (Syria, Iraq, Jordan and Saudi Arabia). Daniel tells us that these 5 nations are given dominion

at the time of the end. Also, these 5 countries only have 4 leaders (heads), which would mean one of them is without a leader at the time they form an alliance. It is not certain which nation does not have a leader. It could be Syria since Damascus becomes a city in ruin around the time of the end, in accordance with Isaiah 17.

How could these five nations be given dominion? The vast oil reserves that these countries contain could easily give them the power to control a world so dependent upon oil. A possible scenario might be for a crisis to develop in the Middle East causing either Israel or the USA to destroy Damascus. These five Arab nations could then form a coalition and turn off the oil in retaliation![3] Daniel's third beast would rise up from the sea!

Of course, this is only one possible scenario. The unstable situation with the nations surrounding Israel could erupt into a crisis at any time, forcing these Arab countries to form an alliance as depicted in Daniel's vision of the third beast.

Once the Arab coalition has dominion, this could be the decisive catalyst for the fourth beast to rise up from the sea:

> *"After this I saw in the night visions, and behold, a* ***fourth beast***, *dreadful and terrible, exceedingly strong. It had huge* ***iron*** *teeth; it was devouring, breaking in pieces, and trampling the residue with its feet. It was* ***different*** *from all the beasts that were* ***before it,*** [(#6925)] *and it had* ***ten horns***" (Dan 7:7).

The fourth beast is different from the other three beasts *"that were before it…"* The Hebrew word *qodam* (#6925) should have been translated as *"in front of"* or *"in the presence of"* as opposed to *"before."* The first three beasts are in the presence of the fourth beast, i.e., all four beasts are contemporary and not successive. They all exist together during the time of the end.

The 4th beast is the most terrifying of them all and it includes ten horns. Notice the 4 beasts also have a total of 7 heads:

Daniel's 4 beasts:	Heads
1st Lion (England)	1
2nd Bear (Russia)	1
3rd Leopard (Egypt, Syria, Iraq Jordan, Saudi Arabia)	4
4th Diverse BEAST	1
	7

Daniel's **four** beasts have 7 heads and 10 horns; exactly the same as John's beast described in Revelation 13:1, 2: *"1) And I saw a **beast** rising up out of the sea, having **seven heads and ten horns**…2) Now the beast which I saw was like a **leopard**, his* *feet were like the feet of a **bear**, and his mouth like the mouth of a **lion**. The **dragon** gave him his power, his throne and great authority."*

Daniel's fourth beast will produce the Antichrist, who will arise forming the fourth kingdom that is different from the other three kingdoms; and it *"shall **devour the whole earth**, Trample it and break it in pieces"* (Dan 7:23). He is also known as a little horn:

> *"I was considering the horns, and there was **another horn, a little one**, coming up among them, before whom three of the first horns were plucked out by the roots. And there, in this horn, were eyes like the **eyes of a man**, and a mouth **speaking pompous words**"* (Dan 7:8).

Identity of the Fourth Beast

In order to identify this fourth beast it is important to look for a world power with the strength and authority portrayed in the verses explained above. Any honest observer would have to admit that the United States and the European nations are prime candidates. Please see Appendix 3 for a review of how the fourth beast is explained in John's book of the Apocalypse, as well as a little-known book from the Apocrypha that was originally included in the Authorized King James Bible of 1611.

Once the third Arab beast is given dominion, the United States and Europe will be forced to take action. What better time for the Antichrist to emerge?

Identity of Ten Horns

In the last chapter we discussed the ten toes found in King Nebuchadnezzar's dream. Some believe they arise from nations in the Middle East; however, Daniel's third beast already includes most of the nations listed in Psalm 83[4] who hate Israel: *"Come, and let us cut them off from being a nation, that the name of Israel may be remembered no more"* (Psa 83:4).

Others think the world will be divided into 10 major regions. This is not as likely since the word for *horn* in Scripture is used to refer to a nation or the leader of the nation.

As discussed in the previous chapter, another possibility would be for the United Nations to increase their permanent membership to 10 countries. This could be problematic, since the 5 current permanent members include: England (1st beast), Russia (2nd beast), France, China and the United States. England and France could become part of the 10 horns; however, the fate of Russia and China may be partly alluded to when we consider Daniel's *fifth vision* later in this book.

The majority of commentators believe that the 10 horns will arise from Europe. We would agree that they probably will be 10 European nations to arise to form an alliance with America in reaction to the appearance of the *third beast* described earlier. This could in some way involve a restructuring within the United Nations (*cf.* Dan 7:20, 24).

The purpose of this book is not to assert dogmatic identities of the nations and events associated with Daniel's visions. The final outcome will be discovered in the near future as history plays out in these captivating prophecies. As noted by one prominent commentator: "…it may suffice to remark that if the prophecy be still unfulfilled, its meaning will be incontestable when the time arrives" (Anderson, p. 277).

War with the Saints

An often overlooked aspect of Daniel's description of the Antichrist (little horn) is his persecution of the saints:

> *"He shall speak words against the Most High, and **shall wear out the saints of the Most High**, ...and **they shall be given into his hand** for a time, times, and half a time [3½ years]"* (Dan 7:25 – ESV).

Those believers who subscribe to the strictly dispensational view of the rapture are perplexed by this verse since they have been taught that all believers are taken away before the tribulation begins.

One of the main purposes of this author's ministry has been to alert the church to this critical truth.   All of the books on our website deal with this important issue: the Lord will deliver His firstfruits (overcomers) before the trials begin; however, those who are not ready and looking for their Lord to return will face this 3½-year period of trial at the hands of the Antichrist.

Daniel 7:21 and 7:25 warn believers that the Antichrist will make war with them, and the Apostle John confirms it:

> *"And the dragon was wroth with the woman, and **went to make war** with **the remnant of her seed, which keep the commandments of God**, and **have the testimony of Jesus Christ**"* (Rev 12:17 – KJ).
> *"It was granted to him to **make war with the saints and to overcome them**..."* (Rev 13:7)

The believers who remain will be given this great test of their faith, requiring them to stand up to the beast. They will be able to triumph over him because Jesus overcame death for them:

> *"And **they overcame** him by the **blood of the Lamb**, and by the **word of their testimony**; and they **loved not their lives unto the death**"* (Rev 12:11 – KJ).

They will learn to be overcomers and proclaim the final victory and get to witness the destruction of the Antichrist:

> *"But the court shall sit in judgment, and his dominion shall be taken away, to be **consumed and destroyed to the end**"* (Dan 7:26 – ESV).

Daniel closes out his vision with the little horn of the fourth beast being stripped of his authority. This will happen at the great battle of Armageddon where Jesus brings God's final wrath. The **beast** and the **false prophet**, who were responsible for deceiving mankind, will be consumed and destroyed:

> *"19) And I saw the **beast**, the kings of the earth, and their armies, gathered together to make war against Him who sat on the horse and against His army. 20) Then the **beast was captured**, and with him the **false prophet**.... These **two were cast alive** into the **lake of fire burning with brimstone**"* (Rev 19:19-20).

The Antichrist will accompany the false prophet as they are both cast into the **lake of fire**. These are the only ones who will go into the lake of fire at that time. The first three beasts (lion, bear, and the leopard) will have their kingdoms taken away at the second coming, while their final judgment will occur 1,000 years later at the Great White Throne Judgment.

> *"As for the rest of the beasts, they had their dominion taken away, yet their lives were prolonged for a season and a time"* (Dan 7:12).

Finally, the faithful saints of the Most High will joyfully enter in the coming Kingdom that will never end. What a glorious hope believers have to look forward to when Jesus Christ returns and defeats all of our enemies.

> *"18) But the **saints of the Most High** shall receive the kingdom and possess the kingdom forever, forever and ever...*
> *27) And the kingdom and the dominion and the greatness of the kingdoms under the whole heaven*
> ***shall be given to the people of the saints of the Most High;***
> *his kingdom shall be an everlasting kingdom, and all dominions shall serve and obey him"* (Dan 7:18, 27 – ESV).

Summary

This chapter has shown that the traditional interpretation of Daniel 7 is not merely a recapitulation of Daniel 2. The four kingdoms of Babylon, Med-Persia, Greece and Rome that are found in Daniel 2 are not the four great beasts in Daniel 7.

Instead, the four beasts in Daniel 7 represent four nations that will arise *at the time of the end just prior to the second coming of Christ.* As we have seen, two of the four beasts have already surfaced (Great Britain and Russia). The two remaining beasts are getting ready to rise up on the world stage at any moment.

The book of Revelation tells us about a great harlot seen riding on Daniel's beast with seven heads and ten horns (Rev 17:1-3). The Apostle John describes this great harlot as the *"beast out of the earth"* (Rev 13), also known as the **false prophet**. As we will discover in the next chapter, Daniel's prophecies also depict this great deceiver during the time of the end.

Chapter 3 – Vision of a Ram, Goat and Little Horn

The vision described in Daniel 8 is perhaps one of the most difficult and highly debated of all the visions Daniel received. Practically all the interpretations miss what God wanted us to comprehend. Fortunately He gave Dr. Wallace Emerson (1887-1987) the keen perception to help unravel the great mystery surrounding this important chapter. What follows is largely based upon what Dr. Emerson discovered. First, the vision needs to be properly divided into sections:

Background (v. 3-8)	Main Theme (v. 9-14)
Ancient History	End Time Events
549–63 BC	(Heavenly Aspects)
Background Interpretation	Main Theme Interpretation
(v. 20-22)	(v. 23-27)
Med-Persia	Time of the End
Greece	Little Horn
Four Kingdoms	(Earthly Aspects)

Next, we need to realize that Daniel's previous vision gave a summary of most of the players involved during the time of the end. Also, we should remember that the Apostle John's Apocalypse included the final word to mankind outlining God's plan. John's visions included two great beasts: *"beast out of the sea" and a "beast out of the earth"* (Rev 13:1, 11), figures for the Antichrist and the *false prophet*. Since the false prophet plays such a key role during the time of the end, it seems highly unlikely that the visions given to Daniel would omit such a central figure.

We will begin our investigation into this important vision by considering the historical background portion of the key nations involved. The following sections of Daniel 8 are presented side-by-side, showing the background along with the interpretation.

Background (v. 3-8) Ram and Goat	Interpretation of Background (v. 20-22)
3) *Then I lifted my eyes and saw, and there, standing beside the river, was a* **ram** *which had* **two horns**, *[Med-Persia]and the two horns were high....no animal could withstand him; nor was there any that could deliver from his hand, but he did according to his will....* 5) *suddenly a* **male goat** *[Greece]came from the west, across the surface of the whole earth, without touching the ground; and the goat had a notable horn between his eyes.[Alexander]...6) Then he came to the ram that had two horns, ... and ran at him with furious power. 7)... he was moved with rage against him.... and broke his two horns.... cast him down to the ground and trampled him... 8) Therefore the male goat grew very great; but when he became strong, the* **large horn** *was broken, and in place of it* **four notable ones** *came up toward the* **four winds of heaven** *[four kingdoms]* (Dan 8:3-8).	20) *As for the* **ram** *which you saw, having the* **two horns**— *they are the kings of* **Media and Persia**. *21) And the* **male goat** *is the kingdom of* **Greece**. *The large horn that is between its eyes is the first king [Alexander]. 22) As for the broken horn and the four that stood up in its place,* **four kingdoms** *shall arise out of that nation, but not with its power [four kingdoms toward the four winds of heaven – i.e., the Diadochi kingdoms toward the north, south, east and west]* (Dan 8:20-22). **Cassander** – Macedonia and Greece (west) **Lysimachus** – Thrace and Asia Minor (north) **Seleucus** – Syria, Babylon, and India (east) **Ptolemy** – Egypt, Palestine, and Arabia (south)

The vision and the interpretation were written around the year 551 BC and they give us a vivid description of some of the major events that took place in ancient history. The **ram** with **two horns** pictures the Median Empire, which came up first and was conquered by the Persian Empire when Cyrus came to power uniting the two kingdoms into the vast Med-Persian Empire around 549 BC. This empire controlled territories spanning three continents for over two hundred years until the **male goat** suddenly appeared.

The angel Gabriel interprets the vision telling us the male goat represents Greece, and we know from history, Alexander the Great is the one pictured as the large horn between the goat's eyes. While Daniel's vision does not provide much detail, we know from history that Alexander's swift conquests were legendary. From around 334 to 330 BC, his fierce military had invaded all the countries from Greece to Persia and into India. This young ruler had control of the entire Near East; however, his rule was short lived.

Daniel tells us *"when he became strong, the **large horn** was broken."* After conquering most of the known world, Alexander died at the young age of 32. His vast empire was then divided into four kingdoms spanning *"the **four winds of heaven**."* The *Diadochi* were the four successors, who did not have the same power or control that Alexander maintained. The vast Greek empire experienced numerous wars after Alexander's death in 323 BC, and no one leader would ever emerge to rule the vast territory again, until the Roman Empire arrived as described in Daniel's first vision of King Nebuchadnezzar's great statue.

Most astute commentators note that one of the most important contributions Alexander the Great made to the world was the spread of Greek philosophy and language. The New Testament was written in the common language of the people, **koine** Greek, facilitating the spread of the Gospel.

Before we look at the main theme of Daniel's vision, we should notice who will be interpreting it for us. In the following, we learn of a Voice speaking to the angel Gabriel. Many expositors agree this must mean God was present, providing the interpretation.

Theophany

*"15) When I, Daniel, had seen the vision, I sought to understand it. And behold, there stood before me one having the **appearance of a man**. 16) And I heard a man's voice between the banks of the Ulai, and it called, 'Gabriel, make this man understand the vision.'*
*17) So he came near where I stood. And when he came, I was frightened and fell on my face. But he said to me, '**Understand, O son of man, that the vision is for the time of the end.**'18) And when he had spoken to me, I fell into a deep sleep with my face to the ground. But he touched me and made me stand up. 19) He said, '**Behold, I will make known to you what shall be at the latter end of the indignation, for it refers to the appointed time of the end**'"* (Dan 8:15-19 – ESV).

Here we clearly are told by the angel Gabriel that the vision given to Daniel relates to events at the **time of the end**. To emphasize this he repeats it twice (v. 17 and v. 19).

In order to properly understand the **main theme** portion of Daniel's vision, we need to recognize what period of time the vision applies to. Daniel was perplexed by what he saw, so God sent the messenger Gabriel to explain it to him. Gabriel stresses that the answer, which he is about to relay, concerns events that will take place *"at the latter end of the indignation,"* also referred to as *"the appointed time of the end."* While the background portion of the vision related to ancient history, the main theme section has to do with events that will transpire at the *time of the end.*

The identity of the Little Horn advanced by expositors:
- o Antiochus
- o Antiochus and Antichrist
- o Antichrist
- o Antiochus as a type of Antichrist

All of these can be refuted by the following observations:

Antiochus was a military man, but the *little horn* will destroy many by peace (v. 25). Also, "It seems utterly impossible to think that the language used; i.e. *"grew great, even to the host of heaven" and "cast down some of the host and of the stars to the ground,"* could possibly refer to Antiochus""the interpretation (verses 23-25) does not delineate the historical facts of the person, methods, or characteristics of Antiochus" (Emerson, p. 146-7).

In attempting to fit Antiochus into Daniel's timeline, countless numbers of scholars have tried to arrive at various solutions to the counts of days in Daniel 8:14: *"And he said to me, 'For 2,300 evenings and mornings. Then the sanctuary shall be restored to its rightful state.'"* While a few come close, no one has been able to arrive at a solution to fit the time period when Antiochus desecrated the temple in Daniel's prophecy. This is one more reason Antiochus doesn't qualify as the *little horn*.

Antichrist will also be a man that wages war as a means of accomplishing his evil schemes (*cf.* Dan 11:38; Rev 13:4, 7; Rev 17:12-14 and Rev 19:19). The *little horn* is described as a diplomat who will be a master of deceit to achieve his objectives; i.e., he will destroy by peace, not by war or force.

Since neither Antiochus nor Antichrist fit all of the descriptions in Daniel's vision, we should examine how the *little horn* seen by Daniel compares to the person described by the Apostle John as the *"beast out of the earth,"* also known as the *false prophet*.

First, we should evaluate the main theme portion, which characterizes the Heavenly aspects of **end time** events along with the angel Gabriel's explanation.

Little Horn (Main Theme – Heavenly Aspects)
*"9) And out of one of them came forth **a little horn**, which waxed exceeding great, toward the south, and toward the east, and toward the pleasant land.*[1]
*10) And it waxed great, **even to the host of heaven**; and it **cast down** some of the **host** and of the **stars** to the ground, and stamped upon them.*
*11) Yea, **he magnified himself** even to the **prince of the host**, and by him the daily sacrifice was taken away, and the place of his sanctuary was cast down.*[2]
*12) And an host was given him against the daily sacrifice by reason of transgression, and it **cast down the truth** to the **ground**; and it practiced, and prospered."*
(Dan 8: 9-12 – KJ)

Little Horn (Main Theme Interpretation)
*"23) And in the **latter time of their kingdom**, when the transgressors are come to the full, a king of **fierce** countenance, and **understanding dark sentences**, shall stand up.*
*24) And his power shall be mighty, **but not by his own power**: and **he shall destroy** wonderfully, and shall prosper, and practice, and shall **destroy the mighty** and the **holy people**.*
*25) And through his policy also he shall cause craft to prosper in his hand; and he shall **magnify himself in his heart**, and by peace shall destroy many: he shall also **stand up against the Prince of princes**; but **he shall be broken** without hand.*
26) And the vision of the evening and the morning which was told is true: wherefore shut thou up the vision; for it shall be for many days" (Dan 8:23-26 – KJ).

[Next, compare Daniel's vision to Apostle John's revelation.]

Description of the False Prophet

*"11) Then I saw another **beast coming up out of the earth**, and he had **two horns like a lamb** and **spoke like a dragon**. 12) And he **exercises all the authority of the first beast** in his presence, and causes the earth and those who dwell in it **to worship the first beast,**...13) He **performs great signs**, so that he even makes **fire come down from heaven** on the earth in the sight of men. 14) And he **deceives those who dwell on the earth** by those signs which he was granted to do in the sight of the beast, 16) He causes all...to **receive a mark** on their right hand or on their foreheads, 17) and that **no one may buy or sell** except one who has the mark..."* (Rev 13:11-17)

Daniel 8:23-25	Revelation 13:11-18
A king	Kingship not stated but possesses kingly power
Fierce countenance	Not stated
Understands mysteries	Power to give life to the image of the beast
Power mighty destroy holy people	Causes all to receive mark and causes to be killed non-worshipers of 1st beast
Borrowed power	Exercises all power of the first beast
Destroys with wonderful works	Does great wonders, fire from heaven
Through cunning casts down truth to the ground; causes deceit to prosper	Deceives earth dwellers
By peace destroys many	By economic control causes starvation (no buying food)
Stands up against the Prince of princes	Exalts first beast; causes all to worship first beast
Destroyed without hand	Taken prisoner at the battle of Armageddon (Rev 19) Cast into lake of fire.[3]

Dr. Emerson goes on to note: "The apparent incongruity between Daniel and Revelation; i.e., one little horn in Daniel and two in Revelation…..may be that in Daniel, the little horn may be used to identify the ethnic source of the man; in Revelation, the two horns are of the lamb, the symbol (in this case deceitful) of innocence and peace and an imitation and travesty of the Lamb of God."[4] The two horns in Revelation may refer to the miter worn by the *false prophet.* The miter has two peaks that resemble horns where *"the two horns like a lamb and spoke like a dragon"* is a figurative reference that ties him to Christianity; however, he speaks as a dragon. The dragon is a figure for Satan, proving he is a deceitful imitation.

From the foregoing comparison we can clearly see how Daniel's **little horn** corresponds with the *false prophet.* When this deceitful individual arrives on the world stage, the world will marvel after the Antichrist and the false prophet as they attempt to accomplish their evil designs. Both Daniel and John have given mankind a description of who these men really are.

Students of eschatology may be wondering about the period of time given to Daniel concerning the restoration of the sanctuary:

> *"And he said to me, 'For 2,300 evenings and mornings. Then the sanctuary shall be restored to its rightful state'"* Dan (8:14 – ESV).

Countless attempts have been made speculating how this verse should be interpreted. Since we have shown that it relates to the *false prophet* and not Antiochus, we will defer the discussion of this important period of time until Daniel's final vision of the time of the end is explained in Chapter 5.

> *"And the vision of the evenings and mornings Which was told is true; therefore seal up the vision, For it refers to many days in the future"* (Dan 8:26).

Chapter 4 – Vision of the 70 Weeks

Please read Daniel 9, which is located in Appendix 4, prior to beginning this chapter:

	Verses
Daniel's Prayer for His People	1 to 19
Gabriel's Answer	20 to 27
Seventy Weeks Prophecy	24 to 27

The date for this chapter was around 537 BC and Daniel was studying the Scriptures relating to the seventy years of exile for his people and the desolation for the city of Jerusalem. According to Jer 25:11; 29:4-10, he realized that their time of captivity was almost over (606 BC less 70 years = 536 BC). Daniel was a devout man of God who greatly mourned for what had befallen his people because of their rebellion against God. He earnestly poured out his heart asking for forgiveness and restoration.

> *"And I prayed to the LORD my God, and made confession, and said, "O Lord, **great** and **awesome God**, who **keeps His covenant** and **mercy** with **those who love Him**, and with **those who keep His commandments**...'"*
> (Dan 9:4)

He realized they had been taken into Babylon because they had not really loved God nor kept His commandments. They had not repented of their evil ways after the Lord had sent prophets admonishing them. Their seventy years were about to expire, and Daniel was seeking the Lord for himself and his people.

He was told by the angel Gabriel *"thou art greatly beloved"* (Dan 9:23). God greatly loved Daniel and He sent his holy messenger to answer his prayer the very moment he began to make his pleas.

*"23) At the **beginning** of your supplications the command went
out, and **I have come to tell you**, for you are **greatly beloved**;
therefore consider the matter, and **understand the vision**:*
> *24) **Seventy weeks** are determined for your people and
> for your holy city, to finish the transgression, to make an
> end of sins, to make reconciliation for iniquity, to bring
> in everlasting righteousness, to seal up vision and
> prophecy, and to anoint the Most Holy"* (Dan 9:23-24).

In answer to Daniel's prayer, the Lord revealed His plans: not
only would He restore His people and His Holy city, He also
gave him a vision that would span over the next seventy weeks
of years, or 490 years. In other words, the Jews were driven into
captivity for seventy years because of their sins, but now God
was going to restore them over a period of 490 years (seventy
weeks of years). This extended period of grace is a reflection of
the unlimited forgiveness Jesus would bring. God's mercy was
alluded to when Peter asked Jesus if he should forgive a brother
seven times. Jesus said to him, *"I do not say to you, up to seven
times, but up to **seventy times seven**"* (Mat 18:22).

The seventy weeks vision given to Daniel is a picture of God's
ultimate plan to bring forgiveness to the entire world through a
new covenant (see Jer 31:31-34).   From the time of the early
church, this vision has always been applied to the Messiah,
fulfilling the six purposes given (Hewitt, p. 253).

Doing Away With Sin[1]

finish the transgression – Israel's sins / Forgiveness of all sins
make an end of sins – Heb 10:1-18
make reconciliation for iniquity – Heb 9:26-28 One sacrifice

Bringing the Good News[2]

bring in everlasting righteousness – 2Cr 5:21
seal up vision and prophecy – Luk 16:16
anoint the Most Holy – Anointing church at Pentecost (Acts 2)

The six distinct things listed were all fulfilled by the coming of the Messiah, who was God's final atonement for mankind. All of these purposes were accomplished during these seventy weeks of years. Gabriel then explains how this extended period of grace will be accomplished.

> The vision is broken down into the following segments:
> v. 25   v. 26   v.27
> 7 weeks + 62 weeks + 1 week (½ + ½) = 70 weeks

"25) Know therefore and understand, that from the going forth of the command to <u>restore and build Jerusalem</u> until Messiah the Prince, there shall be seven weeks and sixty-two weeks; the street shall be built again, and the wall, even in troublesome times" (Dan 9:25).

In order to understand the entire vision, we first need to determine the correct starting point. Based upon the above verse, we must find where *the command to restore and build Jerusalem* took place. The following Scriptures should be considered:

Ezra 1:1-3	Ezra 4:24; 6:7,8
1st Year of Cyrus	2nd Year of Darius
Proclamation to	Reaffirmation to
Build Temple	Rebuild Temple
Ezra 7:8, 11-26	**Nehemiah 2:1-9**
7th Year of Artaxerxes	20th Year of Artaxerxes
Authorize Ezra to	Authorize to Finish
Restore Temple	<u>Rebuilding Jerusalem</u>

There is very little unanimity among expositors over which of the above four decrees is the correct starting point for Daniel's vision.[3] This is easily resolved when we see Nehemiah's prayer for the restoration of the city (Neh 1). God quickly answered his prayer, and King Artaxerxes gave him authorization to rebuild it almost immediately. Daniel's divine vision refers to restoring and rebuilding the city, including the streets and walls during times of trouble. Notice how Nehemiah describes the situation: *"Come and let us build the wall of Jerusalem, that we may no longer be a reproach..." "...half of my servants worked at construction, while the other half held the spears, the shields, the bows, and wore armor; and the leaders were behind all the house of Judah"* (Neh 2:17; 4:16).

Nehemiah's account of his mission plainly shows the *troublesome times* that the angel Gabriel must have referred to. We believe that it clearly aligns with the requirements given in Daniel's vision of the seventy weeks, which places the correct starting point of this key prophecy at the 20th year of King Artaxerxes' reign.   As noted by one eminent commentator: "This is the first and only royal decree granting permission to "restore and build Jerusalem" (Walvoord, p. 276).

20th Year of Artaxerxes

The next major difficulty in ascertaining the point to begin our timeline is determining when the 20th year of Artaxerxes actually occurred. The most popular date given by most scholars is around 445 or 444 BC. This is the time used by Sir Robert Anderson in his famous work **The Coming Prince**, in which he calculated the date Christ was crucified. His book has recently come under attack due to his use of a 360-day prophetic year that one commentator noted was "a mode of reckoning, which was never adopted by the Hebrews, and therefore is so thoroughly destitute of foundation, that we need not stop to prove its incorrectness..." (Hengstenberg, p. 211).

Moreover, new evidence has recently been established that dates the 20th year of Artaxerxes as 454 BC.[4] Dr. Floyd Nolen Jones' significant work **The Chronology of the Old Testament** was first published in 1993. Dr. Jones's painstaking volume gives us a fresh new solution to Daniel's prophecy based upon a modification to the previous work of Ussher's monumental work *The Annals of the World*, published in 1658. With the biblically corrected date of 454 BC as the 20th year of King Artaxerxes, we have determined the proper starting point for Daniel's seventy weeks.

Interestingly, after we uncovered this correct beginning date, we found two older expositors who had previously determined Daniel's seventy weeks should also begin around 454 BC. Albert Barnes (1834)[5] arrived at 454 BC, while E. W. Hengstenberg (1864)[6] calculated 455 BC. These eminent scholars realized this important time well before recent expositors appeared creating unfounded interpretations based upon the erroneous date of 444–445 BC. Many of the traditions taught today were based upon this inaccurate chronology.

Timeline for Seventy Weeks
The timeline for the seventy weeks of years can be found at the end of this chapter on page 50. From the start date of 454 BC the prophecy states we should move forward 7 weeks (49 years) and then another 62 weeks (434 years) for a total of 483 years. The remaining 1 week (7 years) follows the 483 years for a total of 490 years (7 x 70 weeks).

If we move forward from 454 BC by 49 years, we come to around 405 BC. While there are no known records in the Scripture that point to this exact moment in time, Albert Barnes noted: "the completion of the work undertaken by Nehemiah …reached to the period here designated; and his last act as governor of Judea, in restoring the people, and placing the affairs of the nation on its former basis, occurred at just about the period of the forty-nine years after the issuing of the command by Artaxerxes. That event, as is supposed above, occurred in 454 BC. The close of the seven weeks, or the forty-nine years, would therefore be 405 BC. This would be about the last year of the reign of Darius Nothus."[7]

"...from the going forth of the command to restore and build Jerusalem until Messiah the Prince, there shall be <u>seven weeks</u> and <u>sixty-two weeks</u>" (Dan 9:25).

> The sixty-two weeks (434 years) takes us to 29-30 AD.
> (454 BC + 49 years + 434 years = 29-30 AD).

Christ's Ministry

The year 29-30 AD is the time when Jesus began His ministry as recorded in the four Gospels. He was baptized in the Jordan River and He preached about the coming Kingdom for a total of approximately 3½ years, after which He was crucified.

> *"And after the sixty-two weeks Messiah shall be cut off, but not for Himself..."* (Dan 9:26)

Jesus was killed or *cut off* because the Jews rejected their Messiah and the Romans crucified Him on a cross, precisely as the Prophet Daniel saw in the vision the angel Gabriel had explained over twenty-five hundred years ago.

> *"And he shall confirm **(strengthen)**[1396] the **covenant** with many for one week; and in the **midst of the week** He shall cause the **sacrifice and the oblation to cease**..."* (Dan 9:27 – KJ)

Jesus began his ministry that was stopped halfway through (i.e., middle of seven years = 3½ years). Jesus had come to **strengthen** the covenant of love and mercy as mentioned previously in His prayer: *"O Lord, **great** and **awesome God**, who **keeps His covenant** and **mercy**..."* (Dan 9:4)

The covenant that Daniel is referring to is the covenant of love and mercy that God made with his people. Notice what Jesus had to say regarding this covenant at the Last Supper:

> *"And he said unto them, this is my blood of the **new covenant** which is **shed for many**"* (Mar 14:24).

At the Last Supper, the Lord was revealing how the wine the disciples were about to drink represented the blood of a *new covenant*, which was about to be shed the very next day. His blood actually strengthens the original covenant because there would no longer be any need to continue to offer sacrifices to God (i.e., *He shall cause the **sacrifice and the oblation to cease**). His act of love by dying on the cross ended sacrifices and made the original covenant a more durable covenant that would permanently bind His love to all of humanity.

The precious lifeblood of Jesus Christ is like superglue that forever binds God's covenant of love and mercy to mankind. His atonement creates an everlasting bond of God's love that can never be broken (*cf.* Heb 7:22-28; Heb 9:11-15).

Calling Cornelius After 3½ Years
Jesus was crucified in the middle of the seventieth week of Daniel (*in the midst of the week*) after which the Good News of the coming kingdom was preached to the people of Israel. Remember, the extended period of grace promised in Daniel's vision was for seventy weeks of years, i.e., 490 years. After Christ's death there still remained three and one-half years to fulfill God's purposes to the Jewish people. Over this period the Gospel was preached almost exclusively to the Jews.

The confirmation of the new covenant to the people of Israel continued from the day of Pentecost when 3,000 Jews were saved, and as noted by another eminent commentator: "In that three and one-half years it is stated more than once that great numbers of Jews…were converted…one might safely conclude 100,000 Jews were converted and brought to the knowledge of the truth…" (Carroll, p. 133).

But Israel's extended day of grace came to an end when the Jews persecuted the Church and Stephen was stoned (Act 7:54-60).[8] Shortly thereafter, God's program turned from the Jewish people when the Apostle Peter received a supernatural vision. He was sent to the house of Cornelius, where he preached the Word of God and the Holy Spirit fell on the Gentiles for the first time.   Peter then commanded them to be baptized in the name of the Lord (see Acts 10)[9].

Jesus alluded to this same time of 3½ years in His parable of the barren fig tree: *"...Look, for **three years** I have come seeking fruit on this **fig tree** and find none...But he said...let it alone this year also...and if it bears fruit well. But if not, **after that you can cut it down"** (Luk 13:7-8).

Destruction of Jerusalem
Once the people of Israel failed to bear fruit, the final week ended. The seventy weeks (490 years) in Daniel's vision were completed, and God turned his attention to the Gentiles with the conversion of Cornelius.   Since Israel rejected Christ and the Apostles' message, Jesus says the *fig tree* should be cut down.

Notice that the destruction of Jerusalem and the Temple occurs after the seventy weeks are completed. The prince who was to come was Titus who led the Roman armies. Jesus also alluded to this time: *"But when you see Jerusalem surrounded by armies, then know that its desolation is near"* (Luk 21:20).

"...and the people of the prince who is to come shall destroy the city and the sanctuary. The end of it shall be with a flood, and till the end of the war desolations are determined"(Dan 9:26).

Abomination of Desolation
The Jewish people had been given an extended period of grace of seventy weeks or 490 years. They crucified the Messiah and rejected the message the Apostles brought to save them. To make matters even worse, they continued to offer sacrifices in their Temple, which truly was an abomination in God the Father's eyes after they had rejected the sacrifice of His Son.

As noted by Hengstenberg, "The ancient temple is…changed, on account of the unbelief of the [Jewish] people and the murder of the Messiah, from a <u>house of God</u> into a <u>house of abomination</u>, which must be destroyed" (Hengstenberg, p. 169).

Because of this, God had the Roman armies sweep into Jerusalem to <u>desolate</u> the city and the Temple:

"…and for the <u>overspreading of abominations</u> he shall <u>make it desolate</u>, even until the consummation, and that determined shall be poured upon the desolate" (Dan 9:27–KJ).

This shows that the flood of God's wrath against the Jews was because they continued to offer sacrifices in the Temple, which was <u>the abomination</u> that forced Him to send Titus to <u>desolate the city</u>. This desolation will continue until the consummation when the times of the Gentiles are completed.[10]

The vision of the seventy weeks is a magnificent prophecy of God sending His Son to redeem all of mankind. Even though Israel rejected their Messiah, God is not finished with them.

*"**A remnant of them will return**; the <u>destruction decreed</u> shall <u>overflow with righteousness</u>. For the Lord God of hosts will make a determined end in the midst of the land"* (Isa 10:22-23).

*"…that **blindness in part has happened to Israel** until **the fullness of the Gentiles** has come in. And so **all Israel will be saved**…"* (Rom 11:25-26).

In 1948, we witnessed the beginning of the return of the remnant. The story is not quite over, but the time of end is rapidly approaching as we will see in Daniel's final vision.

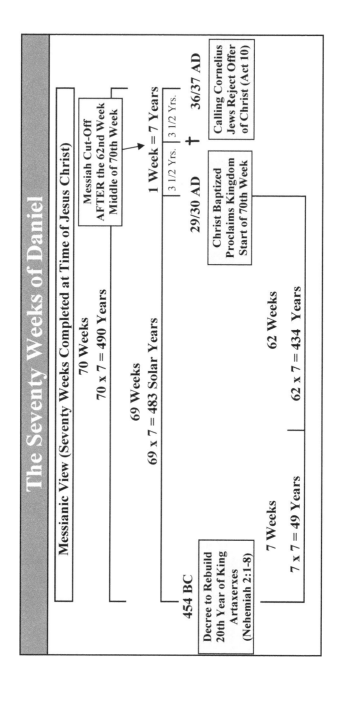

The Seventy Weeks of Daniel

Messianic View (Seventy Weeks Completed at Time of Jesus Christ)

70 Weeks
70 x 7 = 490 Years

69 Weeks
69 x 7 = 483 Solar Years

62 Weeks
62 x 7 = 434 Years

7 Weeks
7 x 7 = 49 Years

1 Week = 7 Years

3 1/2 Yrs. | 3 1/2 Yrs.

Messiah Cut-Off
AFTER the 62nd Week
Middle of 70th Week

29/30 AD

36/37 AD

Christ Baptized
Proclaims Kingdom
Start of 70th Week

Calling Cornelius
Jews Reject Offer
of Christ (Act 10)

454 BC

Decree to Rebuild
20th Year of King
Artaxerxes
(Nehemiah 2:1-8)

Chapter 5 – Vision of the Time of the End

> *"In the third year of Cyrus king of Persia a word was revealed to Daniel, who was called Belteshazzar. And the word was true and it referred to <u>great tribulation</u> (conflict and wretchedness). And he understood the word and had understanding of the vision"* (Dan 10:1–AMP).

Daniel's fifth and final vision was revealed to him around 535 BC, which was after the first Jewish exiles had returned to their homeland. The vision is covered in Daniel 10, 11 and 12 and it concerns the time of <u>great tribulation</u> in the latter days:

> *"Now I have come to make you understand what will happen to your people **in the latter days**, for the vision refers to **many days yet to come**"* (Dan 10:14).

As explained earlier, the term the *latter days* has a dual meaning. When this was given to Daniel it referred to the *first coming* of Jesus Christ to announce the kingdom to the Jewish people. But because God foreknew Jesus would be rejected by the Jews, the *latter days* also represents the time before the *second coming* of Christ.

Our Lord's warnings of coming tribulations also reveal this dual application: *"But when you see Jerusalem surrounded by armies, then know that its desolation is near"* (Luk 21:20). This applied to the siege of Jerusalem by the armies of Titus in 70 AD and it will also be fulfilled in the very near future during the time of great tribulation:

> *"For then there will be <u>great tribulation</u>, such as has not been since the beginning of the world until this time, no, nor ever shall be"* (Mat 24:21).

This time of *great tribulation* that Jesus referred to is also the central topic of Daniel's final vision. This coming time of tribulation will last a little over 3½ years as we will see later in this chapter. This period of time was also referred to by the Apostle John in the book of Revelation.[1]

Before we get into the details of this vision, we should understand the circumstances that prompted it. Daniel was now in his mid-eighties and had been mourning for three full weeks. He was beside the Tigris River when he saw a man appear who was quite different from the angel Gabriel who had appeared to him in Daniel 8. The following description clearly reveals this man as a Christophany, or a preincarnate vision of Christ.

Description of Christ Daniel 10	Description of Christ Revelation 1
[5] Then I lifted up mine eyes, and looked, and behold a certain man <u>clothed in linen</u>, whose loins were <u>girded with fine gold</u> of Uphaz: [6] His body also was like the beryl, and his <u>face as the appearance of lightning</u>, and his <u>eyes as lamps of fire</u>, and his arms and his <u>feet like in colour to polished brass</u>, and the voice of his words like the <u>voice of a multitude</u>.	[13] And in the midst of the seven candlesticks one like unto the Son of man, <u>clothed with a garment down to the foot</u>, and girt about the paps [breast] with a <u>golden girdle</u>. [14] ...his <u>eyes were as a flame of fire</u>; [15] And his <u>feet like unto fine brass</u>, as if they burned in a furnace; and his <u>voice as the sound of many waters</u>. [16] ...and his <u>countenance was as the sun shineth</u> in his strength.

The comparison of the person Daniel saw with the description of Christ in the book of Revelation unmistakably tells us this final vision was delivered by the preincarnate Christ. The men who were with Daniel were terrified and fled away. He was left alone to see the great vision, after which *"8)...no strength remained in me; 9) Yet I heard the sound of his words; and while I heard the sound of his words I was in a deep sleep on my face, with my face to the ground"* (Dan 10:9).

The Person of Christ then touched Daniel and encouraged him:

> *"10) Suddenly, a hand touched me, which made me tremble on my knees and on the palms of my hands. 11) And he said to me, "O Daniel, man **greatly beloved**, understand the words that I speak to you, and stand upright, for **I have now been sent to you.**" While he was speaking this word to me, I stood trembling. 12) Then he said to me, "Do not fear, Daniel, for from the first day that you set your heart to understand, and to humble yourself before your God, your words were heard; and I have come because of your words"* (Dan 10:10-12).

Both the Apostle Paul (Act 9) and John (Rev 1:17) had comparable encounters with Christ, being similarly affected. Daniel was **greatly beloved** by God, and the preincarnate Christ was sent to encourage and strengthen him. He reiterates why He came:

> *"20) Then he said, <u>Do you know why I have come to you</u>? And now I will return to fight with the [hostile] prince of Persia; and when I have gone, behold, the [hostile] prince of Greece will come. 21) <u>But I will tell you what is inscribed in</u> the writing of truth or <u>the Book of Truth</u>. There is no one who holds with me and strengthens himself against these [hostile spirit forces] except Michael, your prince [national guardian angel]."*
> (Dan 10:20-21 – AMP)

Daniel's first vision told us about the succession of powers that would come against Israel: Babylon was the first kingdom, and then Med-Persia followed by Greece. God in the Person of Christ came down to reveal the truth to Daniel about what is to happen to the Jewish people in the future. In the above passage, Christ says He will soon depart to battle with the prince of Persia. After he is defeated, the prince of Greece will come into power. Christ then states that He will show him the proceedings that will take place in accordance with the Book of Truth. "The Scripture of truth is the book in which God has designated beforehand, according to truth, the history of the world as it shall certainly unfold; *cf.* Mal 3:16;[2] Psa 139:16; Rev 5:1" (Keil, p. 423). He also tells Daniel that it is Michael who is the guardian angel over the nation of Israel. It is Michael who stands and prevails with Christ against the powers that want to destroy Israel.

Daniel 11 Prophecy – History from the Book of Truth
Chapter 11 records the vision given to Daniel, which describes (in great detail) the events that would take place in the future. Remember, this prophecy concerns "*what will happen to your people in the latter days.*" These are *literal* prophecies that have taken place as verified by the history books. From our vantage point in time, we can look back and see how amazingly accurate God's Book of Truth really is!

The *latter days* refers to events leading up to both the first coming and the second coming of Christ. Most of Daniel 11 is concerned with events leading up to the first coming. Since this commentary is primarily concerned with understanding the time of the end, it will not explore all of the details recorded in this chapter. Certain parts of these prophecies have dual fulfillments. The literal fulfillments serve as types or pictures of what will take place in the future prophetic fulfillments during the final days before the second coming.

Daniel 11:2-4 – Alexander the Great
> *"2) And now I will tell you the truth: Behold, three more kings will arise in Persia, and the fourth shall be far richer than them all; by his strength, through his riches, he shall stir up all against the realm of Greece. 3) Then a mighty king shall arise, who shall rule with great dominion, and do according to his will. 4) And when he has arisen, his kingdom shall be broken up and divided*

toward the four winds of heaven, but not among his posterity nor according to his dominion with which he ruled; for his kingdom shall be uprooted, even for others besides these" (Dan 11:2-4).

Cyrus conquered Babylon in 539 BC and this prophecy says three more Persian kings will arise before the mighty king of Greece arrives. This mighty king was Alexander the Great, who swiftly conquered most of the known world around 334–330 BC. His reign was very brief and he died in 323 BC. As described in chapter 3 (pp. 34-35), his kingdom was divided into the four kingdoms toward *the four winds of heaven*. None of his four Generals had the same power or authority to rule the vast kingdom Alexander had amassed, and many wars were fought throughout the land.

Daniel 11:5-20 – Struggles Between Seleucids and Ptolemies
For the most part, verses 5 to 20 represent the ongoing conflicts between the Seleucid kingdom of Syria and the Ptolemaic dynasty of Egypt, where the king of the north refers to the ruler over the Seleucid kingdom at the time, and the king of the south refers to the ruler of the Ptolemaic dynasty at the time. These struggles lasted from 300–175 BC with the people of Israel caught in the middle. A detailed survey of these prophecies is beyond the purposes of this study, but for those who are interested, we suggest Jerome's work or Walter Price's superb analysis ***In the Final Days*** (both listed in the bibliography).

The struggles in the Middle East during the third century BC are being replayed during these final days with the two super-powers: the United States and Russia contending for influence and control. America has supported Israel since she became a nation, but Russia has sided with the Arabs who, for the most part, would like to see Israel destroyed. Israel's precarious position today was mirrored in 175 BC with the rise to power of Antiochus Epiphanes, a forerunner to the Antichrist.

Daniel 11:21-35 – Antiochus Epiphanes

> *"20) Then shall arise in his place one who shall send an exactor of tribute for the glory of the kingdom. But within a few days he shall be broken, neither in anger nor in battle. 21) In his place shall arise a contemptible person to whom royal majesty has not been given. He shall come in without warning and obtain the kingdom by flatteries. 22) Armies shall be utterly swept away before him and broken, even the prince of the covenant. 23) And from the time that an alliance is made with him he shall act deceitfully, and he shall become strong with a small people"* (Dan 11:20-23 – ESV).

Seleucus IV Philopator became heir after the death of his father, Antiochus III.   Seleucus sent Heiliodorus to Jerusalem to confiscate funds from the Temple, but God miraculously stopped him (*cf.* 2 Mac 3:7-40). Heiliodorus then poisoned Seleucus IV, but Antiochus IV Epiphanes stood up in the estate of his brother, Seleucus IV.   Antiochus Epiphanes seized the throne by flatteries, meaning he took it by smooth deception, and from 175 BC to 167 BC he severely persecuted the Jews. After a successful military excursion in Egypt in 169 BC, he returned to put down a rebellion, killing eighty-thousand Jews and plundering their Temple (*cf.* 2 Mac 5:15-21). He represented one of the most contemptible and despicable rulers the people of Israel had ever faced. "The persecution of the Jews by this evil tyrant had now escalated to calamitous proportions" (Miller, p. 300).

Abomination of Desolation

His second invasion of Egypt in 168 BC was not as successful, as he was humiliated by the Romans and returned home, where he took out his anger on the Jewish people: *"For the ships of Kittim [or Cyprus, in Roman hands] shall come against him; therefore he shall be grieved and discouraged and turn back [to Palestine] and carry out his rage and indignation against the holy covenant and God's people, and he shall do his own pleasure..."* (Dan 11:30 – AMP).

Antiochus then had a pagan altar dedicated to the Greek god Zeus Olympios[3] erected in the Temple of Jerusalem, creating the abomination of desolation: *"And forces shall be mustered by him, and they shall defile the sanctuary fortress; then they shall take away the daily [sacrifices], and place there the* **abomination of desolation**" (Dan 11:31).

The abomination that Antiochus Epiphanes created was setting up the statue of Jupiter and the sacrificing of a hog on the altar[3]. Antiochus had already desecrated the Jewish religion by forbidding all of their religious practices; this final act made it totally desolate. Not long after this horrible desecration, Judas Maccabee revolted and defeated the forces of Antiochus.

> *"32)...the people who know their God shall be strong, and carry out great exploits. 33) And those of the people who understand shall instruct many; yet for many days they shall fall by sword and flame...34) Now when they fall, they shall be aided with a little help...35) And some of those of understanding shall fall, to refine them, purify them, and make them white, until the time of the end..."* (Dan 11:32-35).

While many sacrificed their lives in this revolt against the Seleucid army, they were successful and cleansed the Temple that Antiochus had defiled. This episode gives us a foretaste of the struggle that will take place in the final days when the Antichrist arrives to persecute the *"saints of the Most High..."* (Dan 7:25) as described in chapter 2 (pp. 29-30). Those who are wise will help others prepare before that time gets here.

Continued on page 60

Abominations of Desolation

Several cases of "*abomination of desolation*" mentioned.

Occurrence	Daniel
False Prophet	8:11-14
Destruction of Jerusalem	9:27
Antiochus Epiphanes	11:31
Antichrist	12:11

False Prophet (End of Great Tribulation)

11) Yea, **he magnified himself** *even to the* **prince of the host***, and by him the daily [sacrifice] was taken away, and the place of his sanctuary was cast down. 12) And an host was given him against the daily [sacrifice] by reason of transgression, and it* **cast down the truth** *to the* **ground***; and it practiced, and prospered. 13) Then I heard a holy one speaking,.... 'For how long is the vision concerning... the* transgression that makes desolate*, and the giving over of the sanctuary and* host to be trampled underfoot*?' 14) And he said to me, for 2,300 evenings and mornings [1,150 days].*[4] *Then the* **sanctuary shall be restored to its rightful state***"* (Dan 8:13-14– ESV). In chapter 3 we learned that the *little horn* of Daniel 8 represents the *false prophet* who will **cast down truth to the ground** (deceive many) at the time of the end (p. 38-40). The *false prophet* will persecute the saints (host to be trampled underfoot), causing the transgression that makes desolate, after which time they will be restored in the New Jerusalem (Rev 21:2, 9-10). This period of 1,150 days will end toward the very end of the tribulation period.

Destruction of Jerusalem (70 AD)

As we learned in chapter 4, the abomination of desolation in Dan 9:27 was the fact that the Jewish people continued to offer sacrifices in the Temple even after Jesus had made the ultimate sacrifice of dying for all of humanity. Because of this, the city of Jerusalem was destroyed by Titus in 70 AD just as Jesus had predicted: *"But when you see Jerusalem surrounded by armies, then know that its desolation is near"* (Luk 21:20) [+ 2nd fulfillment at end of Tribulation].[5]

Antiochus Epiphanes (165 BC)

The _abomination of desolation_ in Dan 11:31 was created by Antiochus Epiphanes when he set up a statue of Jupiter in the Temple and sacrificed a hog on the altar. This abomination took place in 165 BC and was not the desolations Jesus referred to in Matthew 24 or Luke 21.

Antichrist (Beginning of Great Tribulation)

Jesus made another prediction about a future _abomination of desolation_, which He said Daniel referred to:

> _"15) Therefore when you see the abomination of desolation, spoken of by Daniel the prophet, standing in the holy place (whoever reads, let him understand)...21) For then there will be great tribulation, such as has not been since the beginning of the world until this time, no, nor ever shall be."_ (Mat 24:15, 21)

> _"And from the time that the daily [sacrifice] is taken away, and the abomination of desolation is set up, there shall be one thousand two hundred and ninety days[1,290 days]"_ (Dan 12:11).

The _abomination_ that Jesus referred to in Matthew concerns the time of _great tribulation_ during the final 3½ years before the second coming. The Apostle Paul described the leader (Antichrist) during this period as follows:

> _"(3) that **man of sin** be revealed, the son of perdition; (4) Who opposeth and **exalteth himself** above all that is called God, or that is worshipped; so that he as God **sitteth in the temple of God,** shewing himself that **he is God"**_ (2 Th 2:3-4 – KJ).

The Antichrist will cause another _abomination of desolation_ when he arrives in Jerusalem claiming to be God at the start of the great tribulation.

Continued from page 57

Daniel 11:36-45 – Antichrist

The Antichrist is now introduced as the future dictator who God will allow to reign for a brief time at the end of the latter days:

> *"36) And the king shall do according to his will; he shall exalt himself and magnify himself above every god and shall speak astonishing things against the God of gods and shall prosper till the indignation be accomplished, for that which is determined [by God] shall be done"* (Dan 11:36 – AMP).

This man will be unlike any tyrant the world has ever seen and he will rule the world until God intervenes. When the Antichrist arrives, Israel's guardian angel stands up:

> *"1) At that time Michael shall stand up, the great prince who stands watch over the sons of your people; and there shall be a time of trouble, such as never was since there was a nation, even to that time…"* (Dan 12:1).

This represents the time of Jacob's trouble (Jer 30:7) and the time of *great tribulation* (Mat 24:21) predicted by the Lord. The Antichrist's reign of terror will last 3½ years and be unlike any other time in the history of the world.

World War III – 3½ Years of Great Tribulation

> *"40) And at the time of the end the king of the South shall push at and attack him, and the king of the North shall come against him like a whirlwind, with chariots and horsemen and with many ships; and he shall enter into the countries and shall overflow and pass through."* (Dan 11:40)

The final great war of mankind will begin sometime after the Arab nations included in Daniel's 3rd beast arise. This is the leopard represented by Egypt along with Syria, Iraq, Jordan and

Saudi Arabia (Dan 7:6) as described in chapter 2 (pp. 25-27). Some Middle East crisis will cause this Arab league to unite, creating the catalyst for Daniel's 4th beast to come together under the leadership of the Antichrist, who will join forces with the ten European nations described earlier in this study.

The above verse says that the king of the South (Egypt's coalition) will attack him (Antichrist), followed by the king of the North (Russia – Daniel's 2nd beast) joining into the fray. The initial conflict of the war will probably witness Egypt and her allies destroyed by the Antichrist's forces (Isaiah 19). Some students of Bible prophecy believe Russia will also be destroyed at this time (Ezekiel 38 and 39); however, this author believes that great battle will take place at the very end of the millennium as outlined in our commentary on the book of Revelation entitled: ***Calling All Overcomers***.

The exact sequence of the battles during this period is open for speculation, but this much is clear: the Antichrist will be successful in subduing most of his foes since he *"shall **devour** the whole earth, Trample it and break it in pieces"* (Dan 7:23).

Also, Revelation 13 appears to confirm that Daniel's 4th beast is successful in trampling down the Leopard (Egypt coalition) and the Bear (Russia) after aligning with the Lion (England) as one of the ten toes:

> *"1) And I saw a **beast** rising up out of the sea, having **seven heads and ten horns**...2) Now the beast which I saw was like a **leopard**, his feet were like the feet of a **bear**, and his mouth like the mouth of a **lion**. The **dragon** gave him his power, his throne and great authority."* (Rev 13:1-2)

The initial stages of combat will see the Antichrist extending his power over many countries in the world. He will enter the land of Israel and set up his command center between the Dead Sea and the Mediterranean.

> *"41) He shall enter into the Glorious Land [Palestine] and many shall be overthrown, but these shall be delivered out of his hand: Edom, Moab, and the main [core] of the people of Ammon. 45) And he shall pitch his palatial tents between the seas and the glorious holy Mount [Zion]; yet* **he shall come to his end with none to help him**" (Dan 11:41, 45 – AMP).

The book of Revelation indicates that God will protect a remnant of His people in the wilderness during the tribulation period (Rev 12:6, 14-17). Unfortunately, only one-third will be delivered: *"...I will bring the* **one-third** *through the fire, I will refine them as silver is refined, and test them as gold is tested"* (Zec 13:9). Edom and Moab could be the region where they are sheltered because this area will be outside of the Antichrist's control.

After extended campaigns over 42 months, the Antichrist will ultimately be killed as Daniel had told us earlier: *"But the court will sit for judgment, and his dominion will be taken away, annihilated and destroyed forever"* (Dan 7:26 – NAS). Jesus Christ will return with His great army at the final battle of Armageddon to defeat the Antichrist and all of the evil forces of this world (Rev 16:16-17; 17:14; 19:11-14).

Resurrection of the Dead

> *"Multitudes who sleep in the dust of the earth will awake:*
> *some to everlasting life, others*
> *to shame and everlasting contempt"* (Dan 12:2 – NIV).

The resurrection of the dead will occur in two stages over a period of 1,000 years (Rev 20:4-15). The first resurrection will occur after the tribulation period, and the second resurrection of the wicked will take place one-thousand years later. The Lord also taught us: *"...all who are in the tombs will hear His voice, and will come forth; those who did good deeds to a **resurrection of life**, those who committed the evil deeds to a **resurrection of judgment"** (Jhn 5:29 – NAS). Daniel included this warning here to remind us that there will be consequences for how we have lived our lives.

To be included in the first resurrection should be the aspiration of everyone reading this book. Being included in the second resurrection will bring much regret. If the reader has any doubts, please prayerfully consider and read the **Special Invitation** at the end of this book (p. 121).

Count of Days

"11) And from the time [that] the daily[H8548] [sacrifice] is taken away, and the abomination of desolation is set up,
there shall be one thousand two hundred and ninety days.
12) Blessed is he who waits, and comes to the one thousand three hundred and thirty-five days" (Dan 12:11-12).
[Note: words in brackets are not in the original text]

Daniel's final vision ends by giving several counts of days that have remained a mystery, which are shrouded by possible mistranslations. Perhaps *the daily* in the above verse should have been translated: *the blameless[6]*, and could be paraphrased:

And from the time that the <u>blameless are removed</u>, and the <u>abomination of desolation</u> is set up, there will be 1,290 days.

This may be telling us that the blameless believers are removed to a place of safety away from the horrors of the Great Tribulation that is about to ensnare the world. Soon after the righteous are taken away, the Antichrist will arrive in Jerusalem claiming to be God (*cf.* Mat 24:15; 2Th 2:3-4, 7-8). The overcoming Christians are raptured and the Jewish remnant is taken to their place of safety in the wilderness as shown earlier.

The count of days Daniel recorded is probably meant to provide those living during that time a way of determining how much longer they will need to endure before Jesus Christ returns at His second coming.

Shine Like the Stars

*"3) Those who are wise shall shine like the brightness of the firmament, and those who **turn many to righteousness** like the stars forever and ever"* (Dan 12:3).

Daniel's visions were given in order for people to know what to expect during the last days. Now, more than ever, we must prepare for what's ahead. We need to ask ourselves if we are really ready. Just as important, are we helping others prepare?

One wise commentator noted: "The noblest aim is to seek to do good to others…Hence the mission of the spiritual physician takes first place among vocations…The wise man will see that the work…is to persuade men to turn from sin to God and goodness…and the chief honour of heaven is reserved for those who have been wise in effecting the conversions of souls to righteousness" (Thomson, p. 343).

If we are actively trying to turn others to Jesus Christ and teaching them of their need to be living a righteous life, Daniel says we will shine like the stars of heaven! What a glorious day is in store for all those who are actively trying to help others. God will abundantly reward the wise and faithful.

*"45) Who then is a **faithful and wise servant**, whom his lord hath made ruler over his household, **to give them meat in due season?** 46) **Blessed** is that servant, whom his lord when he cometh shall find so doing. 47) Verily I say unto you, That he shall **make him ruler over all his goods.**"*
(Mat 24:45-47 – KJ)

Epilogue

Living in the United States of America, I sincerely hope that some of the interpretations given in this book on Daniel's visions are wrong. We love our country and are deeply saddened to see the direction it has taken. We were once a great nation that was greatly blessed and used by God that has turned away from Him.

Many people living today are in for a big surprise once Daniel's visions begin to unfold. Because believers have been blinded by traditions, they will have a difficult time accepting some of the teachings in this commentary. Hopefully, God will awaken those who are wise that will understand the visions, and they will be led by the Holy Spirit to faithfully share its message with others.

> *"2) Write down the revelation*
> *and make it plain on tablets*
> *so that a herald may run with it.*
> *[or: so whoever reads it]*
> *3) For the revelation awaits an appointed time;*
> *it speaks of the end and will not prove false.*
> *Though it linger, wait for it;*
> *it will certainly come and will not delay."*
> (Hab 2:2-3 – NIV)

We pray that God will use the message in this book to prepare His people to be ready for the times that lie ahead.

Even So Come
by Kristian Stanfill

All of creation

All of the earth

Make straight a highway

A path for the Lord

Jesus is coming soon

Call back the sinner

Wake up the saint

Let every nation

Shout of Your fame

Jesus is coming soon

Like a bride

Waiting for her groom

We'll be a church

Ready for You

Every heart longing for our King

We sing

Even so come

Lord Jesus come

To view a recent YouTube video of this beautiful song, please see our article entitled *Even So Come* on the **Recent Posts** section on our website (www.ProphecyCountdown.com).

Reference Notes

Prologue to Introduction

1) Gaebelein, A.C. – *The Prophet Daniel*, Publication Office Our Hope © 1911, p. 17, "Let us remind ourselves that with the 4th verse of this chapter Daniel used the Aramaic-Babylonian language. It is used by the Prophet to the end of the Seventh Chapter. After that he writes in Hebrew. This in itself is a strong argument for the genuineness of the Book for after the Babylonian captivity Aramaic became the language of the Jewish people. If an impostor had written the book he would have written it exclusively in Aramaic."

Chapter 1 – Vision of the Latter Days

1) Tregelles, S.P. – *Tregelles on Daniel*, Wipf & Stock Publishers © 1852, p. 20, "Now, our Lord speaks of Himself as the "stone", makes reference, or direct citation of, several passages in the Old Testament in which he had been so designated. Thus in Matt. xxi He says, "...And whosoever shall fall on this stone shall be broken; but on whomsoever it shall fall, it will grind him to powder" (ver. 42, 44)....he likewise clearly refers to the destroying judgment which takes place when the stone, now exalted at the head of the corner, falls thus upon the fabric of Gentile power–"it will grind him to powder.""

2) Miller, Stephen R. – *Daniel – The New American Commentary*, B&H Publishing Group © 1994, p. 95, "The Roman Empire dominated the world from the defeat of Carthage in 146 BC to the division of the East and West empires in AD 395...The last Roman emperor ruled the West until AD 476, and the Eastern division of the empire continued until AD 1453." While many expositors show Rome's extended reign, Daniel's dream skips to the feet and toes at the time of the end. The Roman rule over the people of Israel, portrayed by the *legs of iron,* only lasted from 63 BC when Roman commander Pompey occupied Jerusalem until 70 AD when the Jews were dispersed from their land.

Chapter 2 – Vision of the Four Beasts

1) As Daniel's prophecies have been unsealed, a few biblical expositors have begun to see that the kingdoms in Daniel 2 are not the same as the nations represented by the four beasts of Daniel 7. Some of these interpreters include: Sir Robert Anderson, Irvin Baxter, Christopher Bowman, Colin Deal, Raymond Duck, Wallace Emerson, David Hocking, Noah Hutchings, G.H. Lang, Lyn Mize and Edward Tracy. Please see the bibliography for further information on some of their works.

2) The American Heritage Dictionary defines **leopard** as: "1.a. A large wild cat (*Panthera pardus*) of Africa and southern Asia, having either tawny fur with dark rosettelike markings or black fur. b. Any of several similar felines, such as the cheetah or the snow leopard. 2. *Heraldry* **A lion in side view, having one forepaw raised and the head facing the observer.**"
https://www.ahdictionary.com/word/search.html?q=leopard

3) Following the Yom Kippur War in 1973, the Middle Eastern countries led by Saudi Arabia *"united to use the 'oil weapon' against the West. At the height of the war, they announced sharp reductions in oil exports and a complete embargo on supplies to the United States..."* [*Visual History of the Twentieth Century*, Carlton Books Ltd. © 1999, p. 375] Will history repeat itself when another crisis occurs and the Arab countries align to form Daniel's **third beast** waging another **oil war** with the West once again?

4) The Psalm 83 nations include all of the five countries listed in Daniel's third beast. The remaining peoples are the small areas of Gaza and Lebanon.

	Nations Listed in Psalm 83
Egypt	Amalek and Hagrites
Syria and Iraq	Assyria
Jordan	Edom, Moab, Ammon, Gebal
Saudi Arabia ·	Ishmaelites
Gaza	Philistia [Gaza is part of Israel]
Lebanon	Tyre

Chapter 3 – Vision of a Ram, Goat and Little Horn

1) The *little horn* arrives during the *time of the end* from the power that succeeds from the Grecian empire, which is the fourth great empire of Rome. The fact the little horn comes from Rome is verified by the direction he travels: *"...which grew exceedingly great toward the south, toward the east, and toward the glorious land* [Israel]*"* (Dan 8:9 – ESV).

2) While the *little horn* is linked to events at the *time of the end*, there appears to be a double reference to events that took place in 70 AD when Titus destroyed the temple in Jerusalem, thereby ending the Jews' daily sacrifices. The New Living Translation of these verses also seems to imply the heavenly aspects of the *little horn's* future battle:

> *"11) It [the little horn] even challenged the Commander of heaven's army by canceling the daily sacrifices offered to him and by destroying his Temple. 12) The army of heaven was restrained from responding to this rebellion. So the daily sacrifice was halted, and truth was overthrown. The horn succeeded in everything it did."** (Dan 8:11-12 – NLT) "Footnote: * 8:11-12 The meaning of the Hebrew for these verses is uncertain."

3) Emerson, Wallace L. – ***Unlocking the Mysteries of Daniel***, Promise Publishing Co. © 1988. The table on page 39 was adapted from a similar one created by Dr. Emerson on page 151 of his excellent commentary. His wonderful book includes seventeen pages outlining why Daniel's *little horn* is most likely the *false prophet* found in the book of Revelation.

4) Ibid., pp. 153-4.

Chapter 4 – Vision of the 70 Weeks

1) Scriptures for Doing Away With Sin:

"16) 'This is the covenant that I will make with them after those days, says the Lord: I will put My laws into their hearts, and in their minds I will write them,' 17) then He adds, 'Their sins and their lawless deeds I will remember no more.' 18 Now where there is remission of these, there is no longer an offering for sin" (Heb 10:16-18).

Chapter 4 – Vision of the 70 Weeks (continued)

"26) He then would have had to suffer often since the foundation of the world; but now, once at the end of the ages, He has appeared to put away sin by the sacrifice of Himself. 27) And as it is appointed for men to die once, but after this the judgment, 28) so Christ was offered once to bear the sins of many. To those who eagerly wait for Him He will appear a second time, apart from sin, for salvation" (Heb 9:26-28).

2) Scriptures for Bringing the Good News:

"21) For He made Him who knew no sin to be sin for us, that we might become the righteousness of God in Him"(2 Cr 5:21).

"16) Until John the Baptist, the law of Moses and the messages of the prophets were your guides. But now the Good News of the Kingdom of God is preached, and everyone* is eager to get in" (Luk 16:16 – NLT). *Or *"everyone is urged to enter in."*

3) The following is a sampling of a few of the various scholars' views on the starting point for Daniel's vision.

Ezr 1:1-3	Young, Keil, Mauro, Leupold, Calvin
Ezr 7:8	Archer, Hewitt, Miller, Wood, Carroll
Neh 2:1-8	Walvoord, Sir Robert Anderson, Hengstenberg, Barnes, Hoehner

4) Jones, Dr. Floyd Nolen – *The Chronology of the Old Testament*, New Leaf Press © 2005, p. 237. While Dr. Jones does a masterful job in providing the correct date of 454 BC as the 20th year of Artaxerxes, he incorrectly assumes the 483-year period that ends in 30 AD represents the time that Christ died, instead of the time Christ was baptized, as outlined in this book.

5) Barnes, Albert – *Notes on the Bible: Daniel,* Baker Books © 1853, pp. 165, 174.

6) Hengstenberg, E. W. – *Christology of the Old Testament*, Forgotten Books © 2015, originally published in 1864, p. 216.

7) Barnes, op. cit., p. 175. Barnes went on to say, "Nehemiah is known to have lived to a great age (Josephus)….he was thirty years old when first appointed governor of Judea, and that the time referred to at the close of the "seven weeks" (49 years), was the completion of his work in the restoration of the affairs

Chapter 4 – Vision of the 70 Weeks (continued)
of Jerusalem, the whole period would only reach to the seventy-
ninth year of his age....What he did is recorded in Neh 13:7-31.
These included restoring the Sabbath to its proper observance
which had become greatly disregarded...constraining unlawful
marriages...put the affairs of the temple on their former
basis...This was the termination of (their) captivity in the fullest
sense...or constituted a 'period or epoch' in the history of the
Jewish people." God used Nehemiah to restore both the city and
the Temple in Jerusalem during the first part of his life. The
remainder of his life he helped to restore people's spiritual lives.
[Readers are encouraged to read the entire book of Nehemiah in
order to appreciate how the Lord used this faithful man of God
to accomplish the first segment of Daniel's vital prophecy.]

8) Hewitt, Clarence H. – *The Seer of Babylon: Studies in
the Book of Daniel*, Kessinger Legacy Reprints © 1948, p. 263:
"...it is not difficult to believe that, had we the exact dates, we
should find just seven years between Christ's baptism and the
time when Israel definitely rejected the message of forgiveness
by persecuting and scattering the disciples..." Hewitt also
noted: "The last half week is an integral part of the whole. The
seventy weeks measures Israel's added day of grace, and that
day did not end with the Cross."

9) Thompson, J.E.H. – *The Pulpit Commentary: Daniel*,
W.M. Eerdmans Publishing © 1981, p. 274. A similar view of
this time was noted: "the covenant shall prevail for many during
one week." This agrees with the first version we find in the
Septuagint, The covenant–God's covenant with Israel...prevails
with many; "his covenant to send a Messiah...would prevail
with the hearts of many of Israel during one week. If we reckon
our Lord's ministry to have begun in the year AD 30 and the
conversion of St. Paul AD 37, we have the interval required."

10) Hewitt, op. cit., pp. 272-3, "The conclusion seems
inescapable that...'the prince that shall come' shall make it
'desolate,' not for a time only but even 'unto the consummation
of the present age,' Gabriel foretold this final desecration of that

Chapter 4 – Vision of the 70 Weeks (continued)

holy place at the hands of Titus...Such a conclusion of this remarkable vision is both suitable and significant...For the logical termination of the prophecy is the destruction of the city and its sanctuary, just as its beginning was the promulgation of an edict for their restoration."

Chapter 5 – Vision of the Time of the End

1) The Tribulation period shown in the book of Revelation covers a period of 3½ years, exactly the same as Daniel's vision. (Please see p. 72 in our book ***Calling All Overcomers*** that can be freely downloaded: www.ProphecyCountdown.com)

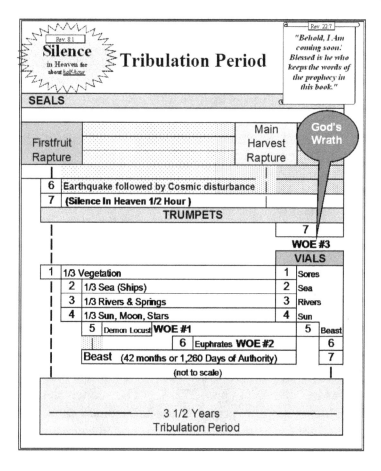

Chapter 5 – Vision of the Time of the End (continued)
2) Keil gives Mal 3:16 as one of the references to the Scripture of Truth. Interestingly, this Scripture is a reference to the distinctive type of individuals written in a special book of remembrance referred to in one of the last recorded prophecies in the Old Testament:

*16) Then those who feared the Lord talked often one to another; and the Lord listened and heard it, and a book of remembrance was written before Him of those who **reverenced** and **worshipfully** feared the Lord and who **thought on** His name. 17) And they shall be Mine, says the Lord of hosts, in that day when I publicly recognize and openly declare them to be **My jewels** (My special possession, My peculiar treasure). And I will spare them, as **a man spares his own son** who serves him. 18) Then shall you return and discern between the righteous and the wicked, between him who serves God and him who does not serve Him.* (Mal 3:16-18 – AMP)

These people are clearly a distinct group of individuals who, we have come to believe, represent the overcomers or Firstfruit believers. As noted above: God will *"spare them,"* which could be a reference to their deliverance, before the tribulation begins, as outlined in most of our writings (see Luk 21:34-36).

3) Miller, op. cit., pp. 301-2. The desecration of the Jewish religion "reached its climax on 15 Chislev (December) 167 BC (1 Macc 1:54) when an altar or idol-statue devoted to Olympian Zeus (Jupiter) was erected in the temple (the abomination that causes desolation) and on 25 Chislev, sacrifices, including swine…were offered on the alter (*cf.* 1 Macc 1:54-59)."

4) Ibid., p. 228: "Most scholars believe that 2,300 evenings and mornings involve only a total of 1,150 days, since the 1,150 evening and 1,150 morning sacrifices…equal a total of 2,300."

5) While the first fulfillment of Luk 21:20 took place when Titus surrounded Jerusalem in 70 AD, it could have its second fulfillment at the future battle of Armageddon when all the nations come against Israel (Rev 16:16-17; 19:11-21).

6) *"The daily"* could be a cryptic reference to the **blameless**

Chapter 5 – Vision of the Time of the End (continued)
believers, whose lives are seen by God as daily sacrifices (per Romans 12:1), and that the *"taking away"* is the rapture of Firstfruit believers (*cf.* Rev 14:1-5). A friend of our ministry recently noted: "What if '*the-daily*', HaTamid (H8548), was incorrectly translated from Aramaic or a scribal error changed the Mem to a Dalet and should have been a noun version of HaTamim, from the same root word, meaning **the-blameless** (H8549) (as a noun, rendered 22 times in NAS)?" This verse could then be paraphrased:

> "*And from the time that the* blameless are removed, *and the* abomination of desolation *is set up, there will be 1,290 days.*"

A reasonable inference from Daniel 12:11 might be that *"the blameless"* are taken away and the abomination of desolation is set up at the same time. This may suggest the removal of the **blameless** believers and then the Antichrist is revealed as Paul told us:"*He who now restrains will do so until he is taken out of the way. And then the lawless one will be revealed*"(2Th 2:7-8). Please see pp. 102-107 in our book **Calling All Overcomers** for more information on the removal of the restrainer.

Appendix 1 – Tradition
   1) Bloomfield, Arthur E. – *How to Recognize the Antichrist*, Bethany Fellowship, Inc. © 1975, p. 94.
   2) Watchman, Dave – *The Truth of Daniel 9:27*, Article from website at: WatchmansTime.com

Appendix 3 – Daniel's Fourth Beast
   1) While many cities around the world claim to be built on 7 hills, the two most notable are Jerusalem and Rome.

Appendix 4 – Daniel's 70 Weeks
   1) Martin, Ernest L. – *The Start That Astonished the World*, Ask Publications © 1991, p. 202, "Jesus was born in a stable, in the twilight period of September 11th, the Day of Trumpets, 3 BC....Then on December 25, 2 BC, when the King-planet Jupiter...would have been seen 'stopped over Bethlehem.' The Magi then went to Bethlehem and gave the child gifts...Jesus was now a *paidion* (toddler) not a *brephos* (infant, as in Luke)."

Bibliography

Commentaries on the Book of Daniel

Baldwin, Joyce G. – *Daniel: An Introduction and Commentary*, Inter-Varsity Press © 1978 [Dan 9C]

Barnes, Albert – *Notes on the Bible: Daniel*, Baker Books © 1853 [Dan 9C] *

Boice, James Montgomery – *Daniel: An Expositional Commentary*, Baker Books © 1989

Carroll, B. H. – *An Interpretation of the English Bible: Daniel and the Inter-Biblical Period* (Available on Amazon or from: www.SolidChristianBooks.com) [Dan 9 C]**

Collins, John – *A Commentary on the Book of Daniel*, Fortress Press © 1993

Culver, Robert Duncan – *The Histories and Prophecies of Daniel*, BMH Books © 1980

Duck, Daymond R. – *The Book of Daniel: The Smart Guide to the Bible Series*, Thomas Nelson © 2007 *

Duguid, Ian M. – *Daniel*, P&R Publishers © 2008 [Dan 9C]

Emerson, Wallace L. – *Unlocking the Mysteries of Daniel*, Promise Publishing Co. © 1988 ***

Fausset, A.R. – *The Book of Daniel* (Available from the Blue Letter Bible (www.BlueLetterBible.org) [Dan 9C] *

Feinberg, Charles Lee – *Daniel: The Kingdom of the Lord*, BMH Books © 1981

Ferguson, Sinclair B. – *Daniel: The Preacher's Commentary*, Thomas Nelson Publishers © 1988 [Dan 9C] *

Gaebelein, Arno Clemens – *The Prophet Daniel*, Publication Office "Our Hope" © 1911

Goldingay, John E. – *Daniel: World Biblical Commentary*, Word Books © 1989

Hahn, Scott and Mitch, Curtis – *Daniel: The Ignatius Catholic Study Bible*, Ignatius Press © 1966 [Dan 9C] *

[Dan 9C] Daniel 9 rightly shown as Christ, not the Antichrist.

* Most useful commentaries in this author's opinion.

Commentaries on the Book of Daniel (continued)

Henry, Matthew – *An Exposition: The Book of the Prophet Daniel*, Fleming H. Revell Co, Published in 1710 [Dan 9C]

Hewitt, Clarence H. – *The Seer of Babylon: Studies In The Book Of Daniel*, Kessinger Legacy Reprints, Advent Christian Publication Society © 1948 [Dan 9C] **

Hocking, David – *Dare to Be a Daniel (Volume 1 & 2)*, Promise Publishing Co. © 1991 *

Hutchings, Noah W. – *Exploring the Book of Daniel: Unsealing the Sealed Book*, Hearthstone Publishing © 1990

Ironside, H. A. – *Daniel: An Ironside Expository Commentary*, Kregel Publications © 1920, 2005

Jerome, St. – *Jerome's Commentary on Daniel* (translated by Gleason Archer), Wipf & Stock Publishers ©1958 [Dan 9C]

Lang, G. H. – *The Histories and Prophecies of Daniel*, Schoettle Publishing Co. Inc. © 2008 *

Larkin, Rev. Clarence – *The Book of Daniel*, Rev. Clarence Larkin Estate © 1929

McGee, J. Vernon – *Daniel*, Thomas Nelson © 1991

Miller, Stephen R. – *Daniel: The New American Commentary*, B&H Publishing Group © 1994 **

Mize, Lyn – *Daniel* © n/a (Available at: www.ffwfthb.org) **

Montgomery, James A. – *The Book of Daniel: A Critical and Exegetical Commentary*, Varda Books © 1927, 2016

Stuart, Moses – *A Commentary on the Book of Daniel*, Crocker & Brewster © 1850

Thomson, J.E.H. – *The Pulpit Commentary: Daniel*, W.M. Eerdmans Publishing Co. © 1981 [Dan 9C] **

Walvoord, John F. – *Daniel*, Moody Publishers © 2012

Wood, Leon J. – *A Commentary on Daniel*, Wipf and Stock Publishers © 1998

Young, Edward J. – *The Prophecy of Daniel*, W.M. Eerdmans Publishing Co. © 1949 [Dan 9C] **

[Dan 9C] Daniel 9 rightly shown as Christ, not the Antichrist.

  * Most useful commentaries in this author's opinion.

Other Works Consulted

Anderson, Sir Robert – *The Coming Prince*, Kregel Publications © 1984 (Original 1894)

Anstey, Rev. Martin – *The Romance of Bible Chronology*, Marshal Brothers, Ltd © 1913

Archer, Gleason L. – *A Survey of Old Testament Introduction*, Moody Press © 1964

Bennett, Bob and Roberts, Mike – *The Wars of Alexander's Successors 323-281 BC*, Pen & Sword Military © 2011

Chitwood, Arlen L. – *Focus on the Middle East*, The Lamp Broadcast, Inc. © 1991

Coerper, Steve – *The "Daily [Sacrifice]" or "The Blameless"?*, Anakypto Forum Article, www.RogerShermanSociety.org

Driver, S. A. – *An Introduction to the Literature of the Old Testament: Daniel,* Meridian Books ©1897

Haley, Henry H. – *Halley's Bible Handbook (Daniel)*, Zondervan © 1959 [Dan 9C]

Hengstenberg, E.W. – *Christology of the Old Testament*, Forgotten Books © 2015 (Original 1864) [Dan 9C]

Jones, Dr. Floyd Nolen – *The Chronology of the Old Testament*, Master Books © 1993, New Leaf Press © 2005

Josephus, Flavius – *The Complete Works of Josephus*, Kregel Publications © 1981

Larkin, Rev. Clarence – *Dispensational Truth*, Rev. Clarence Larkin Estate © 1918-1922. Pictures shown in this book are used with permission of the Rev. Clarence Larkin Estate: P.O. Box 334, Glenside, PA 19038, USA, 215-576-5590, www.larkinestate.com

Lee, Witness – *Daniel: Holy Bible Recovery Version*, Living Stream Ministry © 2003

Martin, Ernest L. – *The Start That Astonished the World*, Ask Publications © 1991

Mauro, Philip – *The Seventy Weeks and the Great Tribulation*, Master Books © 2015 [Dan 9C]

[Dan 9C] Daniel 9 rightly shown as Christ, not the Antichrist.

Other Works Consulted (continued)

Newton, Sir Isaac – *Newton: Revised History of Ancient Kingdoms*, Master Books © 2009 [Dan 9C]

Newton, Sir Isaac – *Observations Upon the Prophecies of Daniel and the Apocalypse of John*, Oregon Institute of Science and Medicine © 1991 [Dan 9C]

New Oxford Apocrypha, Oxford University Press © 1991

Panton, D. M. – *The Judgment Seat of Christ*, Schoettle Publishing Co. Inc., © 1984, www.schoettlepublishing.com

Pember, G.H. – *The Antichrist, Babylon and the Coming of the Kingdom*, Schoettle Publishing Co., Inc. © 1988

Price, Walter K. – *In the Final Days*, Moody Press © 1977

Rawlinson, George – *Ancient History*, Barnes & Nobel © 1993

Rollin, Charles – *The Ancient History of the Successors of Alexander the Great,* Forgotten Books © 2015

Shupe, Pastor Randy – *Babylon the Great*, © 2007, [Pictures shown in this book with permission (pp. 20, 32)]

Shupe, Pastor Randy – *Is America Mystery Babylon the Great?*, © 1988, www.PastorRandyShupe.com

Strong, James H. – *Strong's Exhaustive Concordance*, Baker Books © 1992

Unger, Merrill F. – *Unger's Bible Handbook: Daniel*, Moody Press © 1966

Urquhart, John – *The Wonders of Prophecy*, Christian Alliance Publishing Company [Dan 9C]

Ussher, James – *The Annals of the World*, Master Books © 2015

Vine, W.E. – *Vine's Complete Expository Dictionary of Old and New Testament Words*, Thomas Nelson © 1996

Visual History of the 20th Century, Carlton Books Ltd. © 1999

Whittaker, Harry – *Visions in Daniel*, Biblia © 1991

Woodrow, Ralph – *Great Prophecies of the Bible (Daniel's 70th Week)*, Ralph Woodrow Evangelistic Associations Inc. © 1971 [Dan 9C]

[Dan 9C] Daniel 9 rightly shown as Christ, not the Antichrist.

ABBREVIATIONS

Books of the Bible

Old Testament (OT)

Genesis (Gen)
Exodus (Exd)
Leviticus (Lev)
Numbers (Num)
Deuteronomy (Deu)
Joshua (Jos)
Judges (Jdg)
Ruth (Rth)
1 Samuel (1Sa)
2 Samuel (2Sa)
1 Kings (1Ki)
2 Kings (2Ki)
1 Chronicles (1Ch)
2 Chronicles (2Ch)
Ezra (Ezr)
Nehemiah (Neh)
Esther (Est)
Job (Job)
Psalms (Psa)
Proverbs (Pro)

Ecclesiastes (Ecc)
Solomon (Sgs)
Isaiah (Isa)
Jeremiah (Jer)
Lamentations (Lam)
Ezekiel (Eze)
Daniel (Dan)
Hosea (Hsa)
Joel (Joe)
Amos (Amo)
Obadiah (Oba)
Jonah (Jon)
Micah (Mic)
Nahum (Nah)
Habakkuk (Hab)
Zephaniah (Zep)
Haggai (Hag)
Zechariah (Zec)
Malachi (Mal)

New Testament (NT)

Matthew (Mat)
Mark (Mar)
Luke (Luk)
John (Jhn)
Acts (Act)
Romans (Rom)
1 Corinthians (1Cr)
2 Corinthians (2Cr)
Galatians (Gal)
Ephesians (Eph)
Philippians (Phl)
Colossians (Col)
1 Thessalonians (1Th)
2 Thessalonians (2Th)

1 Timothy (1Ti)
2 Timothy (2Ti)
Titus (Tts)
Philemon (Phm)
Hebrews (Hbr)
James (Jam)
1 Peter (1Pe)
2 Peter (2Pe)
1 John (1Jo)
2 John (2Jo)
3 John (3Jo)
Jude (Jud)
Revelation (Rev)

7-Year Tribulation Period (Truth or Tradition?)

The "Traditional" interpretation of Daniel 9 says:

70th Week of Daniel = Tribulation Period = 7 years

The Word of God does not mention a 7-year Tribulation period. The only one Scripture that does mention a 7-year period is Daniel 9:27!

There are several places in the Word of God that do mention a period of 3½ years. Let's review each of them:

		Daniel's 70th Week ?	
Reference	Time Period	1st Half	2nd Half
Daniel 7:25	42 months		x
Daniel 12:7	42 months		x
Revelation 11:2	42 months		x
Revelation 11:3	1,260 days		x
Revelation 12:6	1,260 days		x
Revelation 12:14	42 months		x
Revelation 13:5	42 months		x

The above summary is very enlightening. It appears that each of the above references is referring to a period of approximately 3½ years. There is not one Scripture that says there is a 7-year period other than the 7-year period of time shown in Daniel 9 as outlined in chapter 4 of this book.

By distorting Daniel 9:27, human "Tradition" has created a doctrine that a 7-year Tribulation period is coming in the future before Jesus returns.

This grand deception has created almost a fairy tale for all who are captivated by its scheme. This author believed and taught this distortion and has humbly repented for allowing this error to carry him astray. The time of the Tribulation period is rapidly approaching; however, there is no 7-year period mentioned in Scripture.

Appendix 1 – Tradition

Paul gives us a strong warning about "Tradition" as shown in the following translations of Colossians 2:8:

> *"Beware lest any man **spoil you** through philosophy and vain deceit, after the **tradition of men**, after the rudiments of the world, and not after Christ"* (KJ).

> *"See to it that no one **takes you captive** through hollow and deceptive philosophy, which depends on **human tradition** and the basic principles of this world rather than on Christ"* (NIV).

Tradition is a philosophy created by man and its effect can be to spoil us and to take us captive. It can even carry us away as a spoil! Some traditions are created and then handed down as if they are sound doctrine. In Arthur Bloomfield's **How to Recognize the Antichrist**, he shared the following insight:

"The only defense against false teaching is truth...(and)...false doctrine is like a disease germ; it sets up a mental block to truth. A person once infected is very difficult to reach. It seems as if one simply cannot get through to him."[1]

Without an open mind and teachable spirit, it's next to impossible to allow the Holy Spirit the opportunity to teach us. We can become so steeped in human tradition that we can't even hear what God's word is saying to us. Jesus warned us of this by telling us: *"Thus you nullify the word of God by your tradition that you have handed down"* (Mar 7:13 – NIV).

Tradition can actually nullify the word of God! The King James version says, *"rendered the word of God of none effect."* By listening to and by following tradition, we can entirely miss what God is saying to us in His Holy Word.

This author has shed many of the traditions he learned when he first came to Christ. Many findings in this commentary may not line up with what you have been taught and you may experience several paradigm shifts in your thinking.

In our commentary on the book of Revelation, we outlined the background of how the traditional teaching on the 70th Week of Daniel was developed from a change in the Authorized King James Bible back in 1885. The following is a brief excerpt from Appendix 3 of *Calling All Overcomers*:

"The time of the Tribulation period is rapidly approaching; however, there is no 7-year period mentioned in Scripture. This popular church tradition is a relatively new one. Dave Watchman wrote on this subject in an article entitled *The Truth of Daniel 9:27*. He notes that the error began in 1885 when the 'Revised Version' (R.V.) was recommended to be the replacement for the Authorized King James Bible by the so-called 'textual critics' of that era!" He then compares the purified Authorized Version (A.V.) with the corrupted Revised Version (R.V.) which renders Daniel 9:27 falsely. The R.V. "makes" the "he" the Antichrist, compared to the purified A.V. text which declares the "he" to be Jesus Christ:

Authorized King James Bible	The Revised Version of 1885
And he shall confirm the covenant with many for one week: and in the midst of the week he shall cause the sacrifice and the oblation to cease, and for the overspreading of abominations he shall make it desolate, even until the consummation, and that determined shall be poured upon the desolate.	And he shall make a firm covenant with many for one week: and for the half of the week he shall cause the sacrifice and the oblation to cease: and upon the wing of abominations shall come one that maketh desolate; and even unto the consummation, and that determined, shall wrath be poured out upon the desolator.

"…the A.V. says '*and he* (Jesus) *shall confirm* (strengthen) *the covenant* (referring to the Abrahamic covenant already mentioned in Dan. 9:4; Gen. 12:1-3) *with many for one week* (7 years),' whereas the R.V. says 'And "he" (Antichrist) will make a firm covenant (peace) with many for one week (7 years)."[1]

His article goes on to point out that Sir Robert Anderson and C.I. Scofield were close friends who used the false rendering brought out by the Revised Version in their classic works: *The Coming Prince* and the *Scofield Bible*. "As time went on, other writers such as Larkin, Ironside, McClain, Pentecost, Green, Walvoord, etc. wrote prophetic books which 'also agreed' with Sir Robert's R.V. interpretation of Daniel 9:27 and formed the basis of our modern prophetic teachings we hear today!"

The modern interpretation believed and taught by the majority of the Church today has its roots in this change made to God's Word in 1885.

Readers are encouraged to try to keep an open mind because some of the findings in this commentary may not line up with what you have been taught. May we all pray for the Holy Spirit to give us open hearts that are teachable to what He wants to show us. May we be careful not to follow the traditions of the past if they do not align with what the Word of God says.

> *"Dear Lord, give us the ability to discern what the truth of your Holy Word has to say to us. Give us ears that will listen and hearts that will understand. In Jesus' name we pray. Amen."*

Beware of Traditions

"Tradition"
One of only five words in
the Bible that have a "Gematria"
that adds up to:
666

"The only defense against false
teaching is truth…(and) false doctrine
is like a disease germ; it sets up a
mental block to truth. A person once
infected is very difficult to reach. It
seems as if one simply cannot get
through to him."[1] Arthur Bloomfield
How to Recognize the Antichrist

"Given sufficient time,
cherished traditions
become dogmatic beliefs."
Amaury De Reincourt

"Minds are like parachutes. They
work best when open."
Thomas Dewar

*"See that no one shall be **carrying you
away** as spoil **through philosophy** and
vain deceit, according to the
deliverance of men, according to the
rudiments of the world, and not
according to Christ"*(Col 2:8 – YLT).

Appendix 2 – The Wise Will Know the Time

When Jesus came the first time, the religious leaders should have been able to determine the time. They had been instructed by the angel Gabriel to "**know and understand**" the timing in Daniel 9:25. Had they studied and applied Daniel's prophecy, they would have known that their Messiah was present! Because they failed to discern these things, they were admonished by the Lord.

> "*Whenever you see a cloud rising out of the west, immediately you say, 'A shower is coming'; and so it is. And when you see the south wind blow, you say, 'There will be hot weather'; and there is. Hypocrites! You can discern the face of the sky and of the earth, **but how is it you do not discern this time?**"*(Luke 12:54-56)

Based upon all of the signs presented by Daniel's five supernatural visions outlined in this book, we need to heed the angel's advice and not make the same mistake people did when He came the first time.

Day And Hour

To ensure that we are not rebuked by Jesus, let's take a better look at what the Word of God has to say about knowing the timing. The most widely used verse people quote when they want to prove that we are not to know when Jesus is returning is found in Matthew:

> "*But of that day and hour knoweth no man, no, not the angels of heaven, but my Father only*" (Mat 24:36–KJ).

What most people fail to remember; however, is the preceding verse: "*Heaven and earth shall **pass away**, but my words shall not pass away*" (Mat 24:35 – KJ).

The day and hour that no one knew about when Jesus spoke those words was when heaven and earth will pass away at the end of the 1,000-year Millennium. The timing of when this will occur is found in Rev 21:1:

> "*Now I saw a new heaven and a new earth, for the first heaven and the first earth had passed away.*"

The reason that this time is not known is found in Rev 20:3, which says Satan is let out of the bottomless pit at the end of 1,000 years for: "a LITTLE SEASON." No one but God knows how long Satan will have to deceive the nations at that time.

Hour You Think Not
The next objection to knowing the timing of end time events is related to the following verses:

> "*WATCH therefore: for YE KNOW NOT WHAT HOUR your Lord doth come. But know this, that if the GOODMAN of the house had known in what WATCH the THIEF would come, he would not have suffered his house to be broken up. Therefore be ye also ready: for in such AN HOUR AS YE THINK NOT the Son of man cometh*" (Mat 24:42-44 – KJ).

On the surface of things, it appears that the Lord is coming as a thief and at a time we will not know. For the answer to this, we need to turn over to the parallel passage in Luke where Peter asks the Lord a very vital question:

> "*And this know, that if the goodman of the house had known what hour the thief would come, he would have watched, and not suffered his house to be broken through. Be ye therefore ready also: for the Son of Man cometh at AN HOUR WHEN YE THINK NOT. Then Peter said unto him,* Lord, speakest thou this parable unto us, or even to all?*" (Luk 12:39-41 – KJ)

In this parallel passage concerning when the Lord is going to return, Luke records a very important question that Peter asks: Is this parable for US, meaning fellow believers, or for everyone? Before we look at the Lord's answer, let's remember why the Lord spoke to them in parables:

> *"Because it has been given to you to know the mysteries of the kingdom of heaven, but to them it has not been given"* (Mat 13:11).

> *"Unto you it is given to know the mystery of the kingdom of God: but unto them that are without, all these things are done in parables: That seeing they may see, and not perceive; and hearing they may hear, and not understand"* (Mar 4:11-12 – KJ).

Jesus used parables, because not everyone is given knowledge to the mysteries of the kingdom. Peter's question about whom Jesus meant in the parable of not knowing the timing becomes an essential point. Now, let's see what the Lord's answer is to this crucial question:

> *"And the Lord said, Who then is that **faithful** and **wise** steward, whom HIS lord shall make ruler over his household, to give them their portion of meat in due season...Blessed is that servant, whom his lord when he cometh shall find so doing. Of a truth I say unto you, that he will make him ruler over all that he hath."*
> *"But and if that servant say in his **heart,** My lord delayeth his coming; and shall begin to beat the menservants and maidens, and to eat and drink, and to be drunken; The lord of that servant will come in a day when he **looketh not** for him, and at an hour when he is **not aware**, and will cut him in sunder, and will appoint him his portion with the unbelievers"* (Luk12:42-46 KJ).

First of all, Jesus says that the *faithful* and *wise* steward will be greatly blessed. They are dressed and *ready* with their lamps burning brightly **waiting** and **watching** for their Lord to return (also please see Luk 12:35-36 and Mat 25:10).

But notice what the **unfaithful** servant is thinking in his heart: *"My lord delayeth his coming."* He is **not** looking and watching as the faithful and wise steward is. Instead, he is beating (Greek: wounding the conscience of) his brothers and sisters. He is saying: **"no one knows"** when the Lord is coming, so "let's forget about it and talk about something else; let's concern ourselves with this present time and enjoy ourselves."

Because of the attitude of the unfaithful servant's heart, Jesus says that He comes for him: *"in a day when he **looketh not** for Him, and at an hour when he is not aware."* To the unfaithful servant, Jesus is coming like a thief. He is going to take him by surprise on a day and hour that he will not expect Him.

The wise and faithful servant will be ready, waiting and watching for Jesus, while the unfaithful servant will not know and will be taken by surprise.

Thief in The Night
This teaching that the wise and faithful will know and the unfaithful will not know is also confirmed for us by Paul:

> *"Now, brothers…about times and dates we do not need to write to you, for you know very well that the day of the Lord will come like a THIEF in the night. While people are saying, 'Peace and safety,' destruction will come on them suddenly, as labor pains on a pregnant woman, and they will not escape"* (1Th 5:1-3 – NIV).

Most people stop reading at the end of the third verse to try to prove their point that the Lord is going to come as a thief. He is coming like a thief, but to whom is He coming to as a thief? Notice what Paul says in the fourth verse:

> *"But you, brothers, are not in darkness so that this day should surprise you like a THIEF."*

Paul is saying that the Lord's coming should not surprise the Christian (**brother**). While the rest of the world will be surprised like a thief, the Christian should not be surprised.

This confirms what Jesus was teaching us in His parables. The wise and faithful steward will be READY, WAITING and WATCHING for Him when He comes for them. The unfaithful and foolish servant will not be looking for Him and will be taken by surprise.

Looking For Jesus
Further evidence for this teaching is found in the book of Hebrews. Heb 10:25 shows that the faithful servant will, *"see the day approaching."* How could we see the day coming if we are not supposed to know? By simple implication, we should know.

Not only should we know, but more importantly we should be looking for Him as taught to us in Heb 9:28 (KJ):

> *"So Christ was once offered to bear the sins of many; and unto them **that look for Him** shall he appear the second time without sin unto salvation."*

This makes it quite clear, Jesus is returning the second time for those who are looking for Him. Further, the book of Revelation implies the faithful will know when the Lord is coming:

> *"I know your deeds; you have a reputation of being alive, but you are dead. **Wake up!** Strengthen what remains and is about to die...Remember, therefore, what you have received and heard; obey it, and repent. But **if** you **do not wake up**, I will **come like a thief**, and you will **not know** at what time I will come to you."*
> (Rev.3:2-3 – NIV)

The church of Sardis was dead. The Lord rebuked it and warned it to repent and to wake up. By implication, if this church will only obey His admonition, they will not be surprised like a thief and they **will know** the time.

The Word of God is very clear. The wise and faithful servant will be looking for Jesus and they will be ready, waiting and watching for Him. They will know the time and will not be taken by surprise.

The unfaithful and foolish servant will not know when Jesus returns and they will not be ready for Him. They will be taken by surprise like a thief and they will not know the day or hour when He will return.

The choice is left up to the individual. He can heed the Word of God and be looking for the soon return of Jesus, or else he can continue listening to the tradition of not knowing and be taken by surprise like a thief.

Wise Will Understand
The book of Daniel ends with words that are prophetic for the time we now live:

> *"Go your way, Daniel, for the words are closed up and sealed till the time of the end. Many shall **be purified**, **made white**, and **refined**, but the wicked shall do wickedly; and none of the wicked shall understand, but the **wise shall understand**"* (Dan 12:9-10).

May Daniel's words reverberate in the reader's ears as they meditate on the message in this book. Many will be **purified** and **made spotless** and **refined** and the **wise will understand**.

Lord, please help us to understand the time we are living in. Regardless of the exact time, help us to be ready and watching.

Appendix 3 – Daniel's Fourth Beast

The identity of the fourth beast in Daniel's vision described in Daniel 7 is found in the book of Revelation, as well as another unfamiliar prophecy written around 100 AD.

Apocrypha

First we will look at the book of 2 Esdras, which is one of the books in the Apocrypha. This little-known book was part of the original Authorized King James Bible (A.V.) in 1611. In 1885 the Revised Version (R.V.) replaced the Authorized Version, and the Apocrypha was removed. While this book cannot be given the same weight as Scripture, we discovered a remarkable reference describing Daniel's **4th beast** of Daniel 7.

> *"...1) I had a dream I saw <u>rising from the sea</u> an eagle...2) I saw it spread its wings <u>over the whole earth</u>...5) and it <u>reigned over the earth</u> and over those who inhabit it...6) all things under heaven were subjected to it, and no one spoke against it–not a single creature...on the earth."* (2 Esdras 11:1, 2, 5, & 6)
>
> *"10) He said to me, "This is the <u>interpretation of this vision</u> that you have seen: 11) the <u>eagle</u> that you saw coming up from the sea is the <u>fourth kingdom</u> that appeared in a <u>vision</u> to your brother <u>Daniel</u>."*
> (2 Esdras 12:10-11)

The above prophecy is over 1,900 years old and it declares the **fourth beast** of Daniel is represented to be an **eagle**! Of course, the **eagle** is the symbol for the United States of America.

John's Apocalypse

Daniel's **4th beast** is also explained in John's portrayal of Mystery Babylon in the book of Revelation, which is described in the following section.

Mystery Explained (Rev 17:7-18)

The angel tells John the clues to solve the mystery surrounding the harlot seen riding on the beast with 7 heads and 10 horns (Rev 17:7). On the facing page is a summary of the key verses, along with this author's speculation of the identity of the nations involved.

Verse 8 – At the time John wrote this, the beast that "was" and "is not" must be Babylon, which fell in 539 BC. It could not be Rome since the Romans came into power in 63 BC with Pompey's occupation of Jerusalem.

Verse 9 – This verse, along with verse 18, reveal that the 7 heads are 7 hills or mountains upon which their headquarters are located.[1] Verse 9 states that understanding the true identity of this important city calls for wisdom. We know these cities will be the headquarters of the Beast and the harlot. Since the city of Rome is well known as *"the city on 7 hills,"* we know this is where the harlot is located.

Verse 10 – The 7 kings include the 5 who have fallen (Egypt, Assyria, Babylon, Persia and Greece, + Rome (which was in power at the time John wrote this), leaving the Beast, who has not yet come (we deem is the New Babylon: Daniel's 4th Beast).

Verse 11 – The Beast that "was" and "is not" is of the 7 that are listed. From verses 8 and 10 above we see this must be from the Beast named New Babylon (the 7th). The actual Antichrist is the *"little horn"* which comes out of the 7th one listed (*cf.* Dan 7:7-8). This *"little horn"* is the 8th and will be destroyed at the very end (*cf.* Rev 19:20).

The Beast will rule from the center of economic and political power. New York City is probably the greatest commercial and banking center in the world. It is also the headquarters for the United Nations, which could host the global government to place all sovereign nations under the Beast's control, in order to bring in the New World Order (NWO). Interestingly, New York will become *"the city on 7 mountains,"* since the Beast will have dominion over *"the seven continents"* of the world. Both the Beast and the harlot (False Prophet) will rule the world from their strategic command centers: New York and Rome.

Mystery of Woman, Beast and 10 Horns

"7) But the angel said to me, 'Why did you marvel? **I will tell you the mystery** *of the* **woman*** *and of the* **beast** *that* **carries her***, which has the* **seven heads and the ten horns***.*

8) The beast that you saw **was***, and is* **not***, and* **will ascend** *out of the bottomless pit and go to perdition.* **And those who dwell on the earth will marvel***... when they see the beast that was, and is not, and yet is.*

Beast Was	Beast Is Not	Beast Will Ascend
Babylon	Babylon	*(Daniel's 4th Beast)*

Beast Was	Beast Is Not	Beast Will Ascend
Babylon	Babylon	*(Daniel's 4th Beast)*

9) 'Here is the mind which has wisdom: The seven heads are seven mountains on which the woman sits.

10) There are also seven kings. Five have fallen, one is, and the other has not yet come. And when he comes, he must continue a short time.

5 Kings Have Fallen	One Is	Not Yet Come
Egypt, Assyria Babylon, Persia Greece	Rome	Beast *(4th Beast)*

11) 'The beast that was, and is not, is himself also the eighth, and is of the seven, and is going to perdition.

5	6	7	8
5 Kings Have Fallen	One Is	Not Yet Come	He is of The 7
Egypt, Assyria Babylon, Persia Greece	Rome	Beast *(4th Beast)* [7 Heads & 10 Horns]	Little Horn (comes out of the 7)

18) 'And the **woman*** *whom you saw is that* **great city which reigns over the kings of the earth***.'"*

(Rev 17:7-11, 18)

* Cities = New York City and Rome: the Headquarters for the U.N. / America and the Roman Catholic Church.

From the foregoing description of **Mystery Babylon**, we see that Daniel's 4th beast is the **seventh** kingdom that had not existed when the Apostle John penned these words. This means that Daniel's 4th beast must be an **entirely new** kingdom to arrive (**it's not**: Egypt, Assyria, Babylon, Persia, Greece or Rome). We believe this embodies America that symbolizes a New Babylon. This new 4th beast is different from all of the other beasts because it is an amalgamation of America aligned with 10 other nations led by the Antichrist (little horn).

Readers desiring additional evidence for America being part of Mystery Babylon should read our commentary on the book of Revelation: **Calling All Overcomers**. This can be freely downloaded on our website: www.ProphecyCountdown.com

We also highly recommend Pastor Randy Shupe's excellent analysis of this subject in his volume: **Babylon the Great**. This exceptional book is available at: www.PastorRandyShupe.com

Finally, as was explained in the beginning of this appendix, we cannot ignore the remarkable description for our beloved nation of America (the Eagle) found in the Apocrypha. While this account cannot be held with the same importance of Scripture, we should not ignore a prophecy written over 1,900 years ago that was included by King James when he authorized the Apocrypha to be included in the Holy Bible of 1611.

While the speculations in this book are not meant to dogmatically identify the various nations associated with the prophecies, we believe God included essential information in his Holy Word to alert believers during the time of the end.

> *"And I heard another voice from heaven saying, '**Come out of her, my people,** lest you share in her sins, and lest you receive of her plagues'"* (Rev 18:4).

Appendix 4 – Daniel's 70 Weeks

Daniel's Prayer for His People

1) In the first year of Darius the son of Ahasuerus, of the seed of the Medes, which was made king over the realm of the Chaldeans; 2) In the first year of his reign I Daniel **understood by books** *the* <u>number of the years</u>, *whereof the word of the Lord came to Jeremiah the prophet, that he would accomplish* **seventy years in the desolations of Jerusalem.** *3) And I set my face unto the Lord God, to seek by prayer and supplications, with fasting, and sackcloth, and ashes: 4) And I prayed unto the Lord my God, and made my confession, and said, O Lord, the great and dreadful God,* **keeping the covenant and mercy to them that love him, and to them that keep his commandments;**

5) We have sinned, and have committed iniquity, and have done wickedly, and have rebelled, even by departing from thy precepts and from thy judgments: 6) Neither have we hearkened unto thy servants the prophets, which spake in thy name to our kings, our princes, and our fathers, and to all the people of the land. 7) O Lord, righteousness belongeth unto thee, but unto us confusion of faces, as at this day; to the men of Judah, and to the inhabitants of Jerusalem, and unto all Israel, that are near, and that are far off, through all the countries whither thou hast driven them, because of their trespass that they have trespassed against thee.

8) O Lord, to us belongeth confusion of face, to our kings, to our princes, and to our fathers, because we have sinned against thee. 9) To the Lord our God belong mercies and forgivenesses, though we have rebelled against him; 10) Neither have we obeyed the voice of the Lord our God, to walk in his laws, which he set before us by his servants the prophets.

Daniel's Prayer for His People (continued)

*11) Yea, **all Israel have transgressed thy law**, even by departing, that they might not obey thy voice; therefore the curse is poured upon us, and the oath that is written in the law of Moses the servant of God, because we have sinned against him. 12) And he hath confirmed his words, which he spake against us, and against our judges that judged us, by bringing upon us a great evil: for under the whole heaven hath not been done as hath been done upon Jerusalem. 13) As it is written in the law of Moses, all this evil is come upon us: yet made we not our prayer before the Lord our God, that we might turn from our iniquities, and understand thy truth. 14) Therefore hath the Lord watched upon the evil, and brought it upon us: for the Lord our God is righteous in all his works which he doeth: for we obeyed not his voice. 15) And now, O Lord our God, that hast brought thy people forth out of the land of Egypt with a mighty hand, and hast gotten thee renown, as at this day; **we have sinned, we have done wickedly.***

16) O Lord, according to all thy righteousness, I beseech thee, let thine anger and thy fury be turned away from thy city Jerusalem, thy holy mountain: because for our sins, and for the iniquities of our fathers, Jerusalem and thy people are become a reproach to all that are about us.

*17) Now therefore, O our God, **hear the prayer of thy servant**, and his supplications, and cause thy face to shine upon thy sanctuary that is desolate, for the Lord's sake.*

18) O my God, incline thine ear, and hear; open thine eyes, and behold our desolations, and the city which is called by thy name: for we do not present our supplications before thee for our righteousnesses, but for thy great mercies.

*19) O Lord, hear; O Lord, forgive; O Lord, hearken and do; defer not, for thine own sake, O my God: **for thy city and thy people are called by thy name*** (Dan 9:1-19 – KJ).

Answer to Daniel's Prayer: 70 Weeks Prophecy

20) And whiles I was speaking, and praying, and confessing my sin and the sin of my people Israel, and presenting my supplication before the Lord my God for the holy mountain of my God; 21) Yea, whiles I was speaking in prayer, even the man Gabriel, whom I had seen in the vision at the beginning, being caused to fly swiftly, touched me about the time of the evening oblation. 22) And he informed me, and talked with me, and said, O Daniel, I am now come forth to give thee skill and understanding. 23) At the beginning of thy supplications the commandment came forth, and I am come to shew thee; for **thou art greatly beloved***: therefore* **understand the matter, and consider the vision.***

24) **Seventy weeks are determined upon thy people** *and upon* **thy holy city***, to finish the transgression, and to make an end of sins, and to make reconciliation for iniquity, and to bring in everlasting righteousness, and to seal up the vision and prophecy, and to anoint the most Holy.*

25) **Know** *therefore and* **understand***, that from the going forth of the commandment to* **restore** *and to* **build Jerusalem** *unto the* **Messiah the Prince** *shall be* seven weeks, *and* threescore and two weeks*: the street shall be built again, and the wall, even in troublous times.*

26) And **after** threescore and two weeks *shall* **Messiah be cut off***, but not for himself: and the people of the prince that shall come shall destroy the city and the sanctuary; and the end thereof shall be with a flood, and unto the end of the war desolations are determined.*

27) And he shall confirm the covenant with many for one week*: and in the* midst of the week *he shall cause the sacrifice and the oblation* **to cease***, and for the overspreading of abominations he shall make it desolate, even until the consummation, and that determined shall be poured upon the desolate* (Dan9:20-27 KJ).

The following chart shows how the life of Jesus Christ fits exactly into Daniel's Seventy Weeks Prophecy.

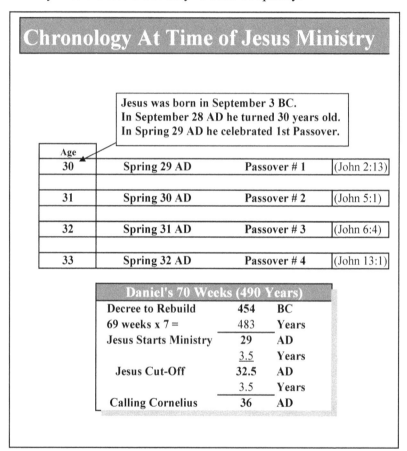

Chronology At Time of Jesus Ministry

Jesus was born in September 3 BC.
In September 28 AD he turned 30 years old.
In Spring 29 AD he celebrated 1st Passover.

Age			
30	Spring 29 AD	Passover # 1	(John 2:13)
31	Spring 30 AD	Passover # 2	(John 5:1)
32	Spring 31 AD	Passover # 3	(John 6:4)
33	Spring 32 AD	Passover # 4	(John 13:1)

Daniel's 70 Weeks (490 Years)

Decree to Rebuild	454	BC
69 weeks x 7 =	483	Years
Jesus Starts Ministry	29	AD
	3.5	Years
Jesus Cut-Off	32.5	AD
	3.5	Years
Calling Cornelius	36	AD

Best evidence shows that Jesus was probably born in September 3 BC.[1] Jesus began his ministry when he was about 30 years old (Luk 3:23). Since he would have turned 30 in September 28 AD his first Passover would have taken place in 29 AD and He would have been crucified 3½ years later. The next 3½ years the Apostles preached the Good News to the Jews until they finally rejected it and God turned His attention to the Gentiles. If we add the 483 years (69 weeks) to these two 3½ year periods we have a total of 490 years in Daniel's magnificent prophecy.

New Tradition Changes Meaning

From the time of the early church, Daniel's Seventy Weeks Prophecy has applied to Jesus Christ being the one to fulfill the prophecy (Messianic view). In recent days new contemporary interpretations have surfaced, which have captivated the masses with a new "tradition" that has become modern church dogma.

This author's original view of eschatology was firmly indoctrinated into believing this new tradition. Being a CPA, I was fascinated by the precision Sir Robert Anderson created in his book *The Coming Prince*, which is considered the standard volume in the field and followed by most in today's church. Anderson was a former Chief of Criminal Investigation in Scotland Yard who studied and wrote extensively, particularly on the subject of prophecy.

His book gives very detailed and complex calculations, which appear to give convincing "proof" that Daniel's prophecy predicted the exact day Christ was crucified. Because of this, Anderson's work has become the "gold standard" for people to go to on the book of Daniel.

As we illustrate in Appendix 1 (pages 82-83), Anderson's interpretation inserts the Antichrist in Daniel 9:27, instead of Jesus Christ as we have explained in this book. This changes the entire meaning of Daniel's magnificent vision and distorts the true significance of this important prophecy. Instead of being about the wonderful story of how God sent His Son to provide Israel an extended period of grace over a period of 490 years, the prophecy becomes a fabricated tale about the Antichrist coming to make a "7 year" peace treaty and then breaking it in the middle of it! This story has become the modern staple for the church today, blinding everyone from seeing the beautiful story Daniel was given.

Analysis of Anderson's *The Coming Prince*

The basis of most of today's eschatology was arrived at through the influence of Sir Robert Anderson and C.I. Scofield. Anderson's work was based upon <u>three</u> erroneous assumptions: an incorrect starting date, the use of a corrupted version of Scripture and the manipulation of dates through a faulty mode of reckoning.

Incorrect Starting Date

While Anderson begins his calculation of Daniel's seventy weeks with the correct decree of Artaxerxes' reign, the 20th year of the King did not occur in 445 BC, but in the year 454 BC as discovered by Dr. Floyd Jones (see p. 44).

Corrupted Scripture

Instead of using the Authorized King James Bible of 1611, Anderson used the corrupted Revised Version of the Bible that came out in 1885. This incorrect rendering replaces Jesus Christ with the Antichrist, thereby <u>changing the entire meaning</u> of Daniel's prophecy. This flawed change has created today's teaching that has permeated most Bibles and books on prophecy. Anderson's work is now a cherished tradition that is dogmatically believed by almost everyone.

Faulty Reckoning

After beginning with an incorrect start date, Anderson used a 360-day lunar year to arrive at his conclusions (see page 44). Instead of calculating Daniel's seventy weeks based upon our normal solar year of 365 days, he was forced to essentially manipulate the numbers to arrive at his solution!

Today's "traditional" teaching has created a faulty scenario where the Church is "Raptured" away before the Antichrist comes to make a 7-year peace treaty with Israel. We find it extremely interesting that the word *Tradition* has a Gematria that totals: 666! In light of the findings in this book, which show the true meaning of Daniel's vision, readers are encouraged to seriously reconsider Anderson's work.

Appendix 5 – Sir Isaac Newton on the 70 Weeks

Sir Isaac Newton had a unique take on Daniel 9, which is not understood by most in today's Church; however, we believe Newton could be correct. If he is, then what you are about to read may be extremely important.

Newton believed that Daniel was telling us the time of Christ's first coming, as well as the timing of His second coming. The chart of Daniel's seventy weeks that follows shows the starting point of 454 BC based upon Dr. Floyd Nolen Jones finding in his book: *The Chronology of the Old Testament.* The prophecy then moves forward 483 years (69 weeks) and ends with the time that Christ was baptized. Three and one-half years later Jesus was crucified (cut off), which was half way through the 70th week. The next 3½ years of the 70th week the Good News was preached to the Jews until they finally rejected Christ and an angel appeared to Cornelius, which began the calling of the Gentiles as described in Acts 10 (see Isa 65:1-7; 66:1-4).

As outlined on the chart at the end of this Appendix, Newton believed that Daniel's prophecy pointed to both the first and second coming of Christ. He believed that Jesus came the first time after the 62 weeks and that Christ's second coming would be preceded by a 49 year (7 weeks) period, which would begin with a decree to rebuild Jerusalem. Shortly after Israel recaptured the city in 1967, the Knesset formed the JQDC for the reconstruction of the Old City of Jerusalem in 1969. Information on this company is also included on our website.

Interestingly, Newton predicted: "About the time of the end, a body of men will be raised up who will turn their attention to the Prophecies, and insist upon their literal interpretation, in the midst of much clamor and opposition." Newton's keen insight into Daniel's prophecies may be the greatest contribution he ever made!

We believe Sir Isaac Newton's interpretation could be correct. Newton was telling us that the final seven weeks would be associated with Sabbath years, but we do not know exactly when the next Sabbath year is. Precisely when Christ will return is not known for certain, but if Newton's findings are right then there may be very little time before the Lord comes for His faithful, watching bride. If Newton were alive today, we believe he would remind us to always remember to "*let time be the Interpreter.*"

The religious leaders should have been able to determine the time when Jesus came the first time. They were even instructed by the angel Gabriel to "***know and understand***" the timing in Daniel 9:25! Had they studied and applied Daniel's prophecy they would have known that their Messiah was present! Because they failed to discern these things they were admonished by the Lord.

> "*Whenever you see a cloud rising out of the west, immediately you say, 'A shower is coming'; and so it is. And when you see the south wind blow, you say, 'There will be hot weather'; and there is. "Hypocrites! You can discern the face of the sky and of the earth,* **but how is it you do not discern this time?**"(Luke 12:54-56)

If Sir Isaac Newton's interpretation is correct about Christ's second coming, we need to make sure we don't make the same mistake people did when He came the first time.

While Newton's chart includes recent dates, its purpose is not to set dates for the Lord's return. Back in 1988 Grant Jeffery's best selling prophecy book: ***Armageddon Appointment with Destiny*** similarly had numerous charts showing the end coming around the year 2000. Since we don't know if Newton's interpretation is correct, we are including his interpretation so Jesus doesn't tell us: ***but how is it you do not discern this time?***

The following represents Sir Isaac Newton's interpretation:

Of the Prophecy of the Seventy Weeks by *Sir Isaac Newton*

The Vision of the Image composed of four Metals was given first to *Nebuchadnezzar*, and then to *Daniel* in a dream: and *Daniel* began then to be celebrated for revealing of secrets, *Ezek.* xxviii. 3. The Vision of the four Beasts, and of *the Son of man* coming in the clouds of heaven, was also given to *Daniel* in a dream. That of the Ram and the He-Goat appeared to him in the day time, when he was by the bank of the river *Ulay*; and was explained to him by the prophetic Angel *Gabriel*. It concerns the *Prince of the host*, and the *Prince of Princes*: and now in the first year of *Darius* the *Mede* over *Babylon*, the same prophetic Angel appears to *Daniel* again, and explains to him what is meant by the *Son of man*, by the *Prince of the host*, and the *Prince of Princes*. The Prophecy of the *Son of man* coming in the clouds of heaven relates to the second coming of *Christ*; that of the *Prince of the host* relates to his first coming: and this Prophecy of the *Messiah*, in explaining them, relates to both comings, and assigns the times thereof.

This Prophecy, like all the rest of *Daniel*'s, consists of two parts, an introductory Prophecy and an explanation thereof; the whole I thus translate and interpret.

> "*Seventy weeks are cut out upon thy people, and upon thy holy city, to finish transgression, and to make an end of sins, to expiate iniquity, and to bring in everlasting righteousness, to consummate the Vision and the Prophet, and to anoint the most Holy.*

> '*Know also and understand, that from the going forth of the commandment to cause to return and to build* Jerusalem, *unto the Anointed the Prince, shall be seven weeks.*

'Yet threescore and two weeks shall it return, and the street be built and the wall; but in troublesome times: and after the threescore and two weeks, the Anointed shall be cut off, and it shall not be his; but the people of a Prince to come shall destroy the city and the sanctuary: and the end thereof shall be with a flood, and unto the end of the war, desolations are determined.

'Yet shall he confirm the covenant with many for one week: and in half a week he shall cause the sacrifice and oblation to cease: and upon a wing of abominations he shall make it desolate, even until the consummation, and that which is determined be poured upon the desolate.'

Seventy weeks are cut out upon thy people, and upon thy holy city, to finish transgression, &c. Here, by putting a week for seven years, are reckoned 490 years from the time that the dispersed *Jews* should be re-incorporated into a people and a holy city, until the death and resurrection of *Christ*; whereby *transgression should be finished, and sins ended, iniquity be expiated, and everlasting righteousness brought in, and this Vision be accomplished, and the Prophet consummated*, that Prophet whom the *Jews* expected; and whereby *the most Holy* should be *anointed*, he who is therefore in the next words called the *Anointed*, that is, the *Messiah*, or the *Christ*. For by joining the accomplishment of the vision with the expiation of sins, the 490 years are ended with the death of *Christ*. Now the dispersed *Jews* became a people and city when they first returned into a polity or body politick; and this was in the seventh year of *Artaxerxes Longimanus*, when *Ezra* returned with a body of *Jews* from captivity, and revived the *Jewish* worship; and by the King's commission created Magistrates in all the land, to judge and govern the people according to the laws of God and the King, *Ezra* vii. 25. There were but two returns from captivity, *Zerubbabel*'s and *Ezra*'s; in *Zerubbabel*'s they had only the commission to build the Temple, in *Ezra*'s they first became a polity or city by a government of their own. Now the years of this *Artaxerxes* began about two or three months after the summer solstice, and his seventh year fell in with the third year of the eightieth *Olympiad*; and the latter part thereof, wherein *Ezra* went up to *Jerusalem*, was in the year of the *Julian Period* 4257. **Count the time from thence to the death of *Christ*, and you will find it just 490 years.(a)** If you count in *Judaic* years commencing in autumn, and date the reckoning from the first autumn after *Ezra*'s coming to *Jerusalem*, when he put the King's decree in execution; the death of *Christ* will fall on the year of the *Julian Period 4747*, *Anno Domini* 34 **(b)** and the weeks will be *Judaic* weeks, ending with sabbatical years; and this I take to be the truth: but if you had rather place the death of *Christ* in the year before, as is commonly done, you may take the year of *Ezra*'s journey into the reckoning.

 (a) 4257 BC to 32 AD = 490 Years*** (see page 108)
 (b) Should be 4745 or 32 AD

Know also and understand, that from the going forth of the commandment to cause to return and to build Jerusalem*, unto the Anointed the Prince, shall be seven weeks.* The former part of the Prophecy related to the first coming of *Christ*, being dated to his coming as a Prophet; this being dated to his coming to be Prince or King, seems to relate to his second coming. There, the Prophet was consummate, and the most holy anointed: here, he that was anointed comes to be Prince and to reign. For *Daniel*'s Prophecies reach to the end of the world; and there is scarce a Prophecy in the Old Testament concerning *Christ*, which doth not in something or other relate to his second coming. If divers of the ancients, as *Irenæus*, *Julius Africanus*, *Hippolytus* the martyr, and *Apollinaris* Bishop of *Laodicea*, applied the half week to the times of *Antichrist*; why may not we, by the same liberty of interpretation, apply the seven weeks to the time when *Antichrist* shall be destroyed by the brightness of *Christ*'s coming?

The *Israelites* in the days of the ancient Prophets, when the ten Tribes were led into captivity, expected a double return; and that at the first the *Jews* should build a new Temple inferior to *Solomon*'s, until the time of that age should be fulfilled; and afterwards they should return from all places of their captivity, and build *Jerusalem* and the Temple gloriously, *Tobit* xiv. 4, 5, 6: and to express the glory and excellence of this city, it is figuratively said to be built of precious stones, *Tobit* xiii. 16, 17, 18. *Isa.* liv. 11, 12. *Rev.* xi. and called the *New Jerusalem*, the *Heavenly Jerusalem*, the *Holy City*, the *Lamb's Wife*, the *City of the Great King*, the *City into which the Kings of the earth do bring their glory and honor*.

Now while such a return from captivity was the expectation of *Israel*, even before the times of *Daniel*, I know not why *Daniel* should omit it in his Prophecy. This part of the Prophecy being therefore not yet fulfilled, I shall not attempt a particular interpretation of it, but content myself with observing, that as the **_seventy_** and the **_sixty two weeks_** were **_Jewish_** weeks, **ending with sabbatical years;** so the **_seven weeks_** are the compass of a **_Jubilee_**, and begin and end with actions proper for a *Jubilee*, and of the highest nature for which a *Jubilee* can be kept: and that since *the **commandment to return and to build** Jerusalem*, **precedes the _Messiah the Prince_ 49 years**; it may perhaps come forth not from the *Jews* themselves, but from some other kingdom friendly to them, and precede their return from captivity, and give occasion to it; and lastly, that this rebuilding of *Jerusalem* and the waste places of *Judah* is predicted in *Micah* vii. 11. *Amos* ix. 11, 14. *Ezek.* xxxvi. 33, 35, 36, 38. *Isa.* liv. 3, 11, 12. lv. 12. lxi. 4. lxv. 18, 21,22. and *Tobit* xiv. 5. and that the return from captivity and coming of the *Messiah* and his kingdom are described in *Daniel* vii. *Rev.* xix. *Acts* i. *Mat.* xxiv. *Joel* iii. *Ezek.* xxxvi. xxxvii. *Isa.* lx. lxii. lxiii. lxv. and lxvi. and many other places of scripture. The manner I know not.

Let time be the Interpreter.

*Yet **threescore and two weeks** shall it return, and the street be built and the wall, but in troublesome times: and **after the threescore and two weeks** the* **Messiah** *shall be cut off, and it shall not be his; but the people of a Prince to come shall destroy the city and the sanctuary.*

Having foretold **both comings of** *Christ*, and dated the last from their returning and building *Jerusalem*; to prevent the applying that to the building *Jerusalem* by *Nehemiah*, he distinguishes this from that, by saying that from this period to the *Anointed* shall be, **not seven weeks**, but **threescore and two weeks,** and this not in prosperous but in troublesome times; and at the end of these Weeks the *Messiah* shall not be the Prince of the *Jews*, but be cut off; and *Jerusalem* not be his, but the city and sanctuary be destroyed. Now *Nehemiah* came to *Jerusalem* in the 20th year of this same *Artaxerxes*, while *Ezra* still continued there, *Nehem.* xii. 36, and found the city lying waste, and the houses and wall unbuilt, *Nehem.* ii. 17. vii. 4, and finished the wall the 25th day of the month *Elul*, *Nehem.* vi. 15, in the 28th year of the King, that is, in *September* in the year of the *Julian Period* 4278. **Count now from this year threescore and two weeks of years, that is 434 years,** and the reckoning will end in *September* in the year **of the** *Julian Period* **4712** which is the year in which *Christ* **was born, (c) 3 BC** according to *Clemens Alexandrinus, Irenæus, Eusebius, Epiphanius, Jerome, Orosius, Cassiodorus,* and other ancients; and this was the general opinion, till *Dionysius Exiguus* invented the vulgar account, in which *Christ's* birth is placed two years later. If with some you reckon that *Christ* was born three or four years before the vulgar account, yet his birth will fall in the latter part of the last week, which is enough. How after these weeks *Christ* was cut off and the city and sanctuary destroyed by the *Romans*, is well known.

(c) 4278 BC to 3 BC = 434 Years (62 x 7)

Yet shall he confirm the covenant with many for one week. He kept it, notwithstanding his death, till the rejection of the *Jews*, and calling of *Cornelius* and the *Gentiles* in the seventh year after his passion. **(***490 years end here)**

And in half a week he shall cause the sacrifice and oblation to cease; that is, by the war of the *Romans* upon the *Jews*: which war, after some commotions, began in the 13th year of *Nero*, **AD 67,** in the spring, when *Vespasian* with an army invaded them; and ended in the second year of *Vespasian*, **AD 70**, in the autumn, *Sept.* 7, when *Titus* took the city, having burnt the Temple 27 days before: so that it **lasted three years and an half.** *And upon a wing of abominations he shall cause desolation, even until the consummation, and that which is determined be poured upon the desolate.* The Prophets, in representing kingdoms by Beasts and Birds, put their wings stretch out over any country for their armies sent out to invade and rule over that country. Hence a wing of abominations is an army of false Gods: for an abomination is often put in scripture for a false God; as where *Chemosh* is called the abomination of *Moab*, and *Molech* the abomination of *Ammon*. **The meaning therefore is, that the people of a Prince to come shall destroy the sanctuary, and abolish the daily worship of the true God, and overspread the land with an army of false gods**; and by setting up their dominion and worship, cause desolation to the *Jews*, until the times of the *Gentiles* be fulfilled. For *Christ* tells us, that the abomination of desolation spoken of by *Daniel* was to be set up in the times of the *Roman Empire*, *Matthew.* xxiv. 15.

Thus have we in this short Prophecy, a prediction of all the main periods relating to the coming of the *Messiah*; **the time of his birth**, **that of his death**, **that of the rejection of the *Jews*,** the **duration of the *Jewish* war** whereby he caused **the city and sanctuary to be destroyed,** and the **time of his second coming**: and so the interpretation here given is more full and complete and adequate to the design, than if we should restrain it to his first coming only, as Interpreters usually do.

We avoid also the doing violence to the language of *Daniel*, by taking the *__seven weeks__* and *__sixty two weeks__* for one number. Had that been *Daniel*'s meaning, he would have said *__sixty and nine weeks__*, and **not** *seven weeks* and *sixty two weeks*, **a way of numbering used by no nation.** In our way the years are *Jewish Luni-solar years*, as they ought to be; and the *seventy weeks of years* are *Jewish weeks* ending with *sabbatical years*, which is very remarkable. For **they end either** with the **year of the birth** of *Christ*, two years before the vulgar account, or with the **year of his death,** or with the **seventh year after it**: all which are *sabbatical years*. Others either count by Lunar years, or by weeks not *Judaic*: and, which is worst, they ground their interpretations on erroneous Chronology, excepting the opinion of *Funccius* about the *seventy weeks*, which is the same with ours. For they place *Ezra* and *Nehemiah* in the reign of *rtaxerxes Mnemon*, and the building of the Temple in the reign of *Darius Nothus*, and date the weeks of *Daniel* from those two reigns.

NOTES:
(a) 4257 BC to 32 AD = 490 Years
(b) 4745 = 32 AD (not 4747 or 34 AD)
(c) 4278 BC to 3 BC = 434 Years (62 x 7)

Regarding Newton's perception of how God was working in the lives of men in revealing truths from the Word of God, Newton wrote:

> "Amongst the Interpreters of the last age there is scarce one of note who hath not made some discovery worth knowing: and thence I seem to gather that God is about opening these mysteries.
> The success of others put me upon considering it; and if I have done any thing which may be useful to following writers, I have my design."

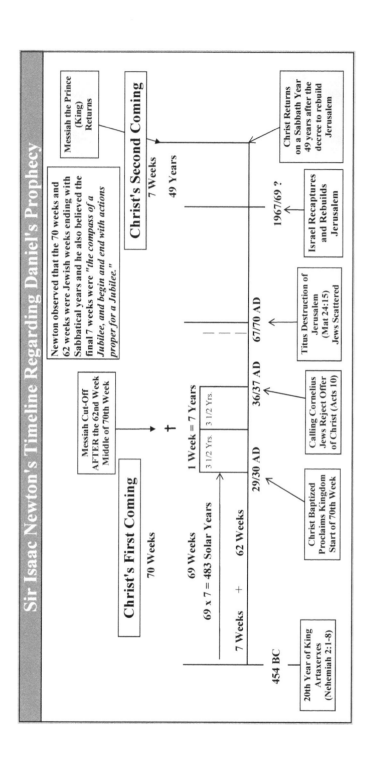

Sir Isaac Newton's Timeline Regarding Daniel's Prophecy

Newton observed that the 70 weeks and 62 weeks were Jewish weeks ending with Sabbatical years and he also believed the final 7 weeks were *"the compass of a Jubilee, and begin and end with actions proper for a Jubilee."*

Christ's First Coming

Christ's Second Coming

Messiah the Prince (King) Returns

Christ Returns on a Sabbath Year 49 years after the decree to rebuild Jerusalem

70 Weeks

7 Weeks

49 Years

Messiah Cut-Off AFTER the 62nd Week Middle of 70th Week

69 Weeks

69 x 7 = 483 Solar Years

62 Weeks

1 Week = 7 Years

3 1/2 Yrs. | 3 1/2 Yrs.

7 Weeks   +

Israel Recaptures and Rebuilds Jerusalem

1967/69 ?

Titus Destruction of Jerusalem (Mat 24:15) Jews Scattered

67/70 AD

Calling Cornelius Jews Reject Offer of Christ (Acts 10)

36/37 AD

Christ Baptized Proclaims Kingdom Start of 70th Week

29/30 AD

20th Year of King Artaxerxes (Nehemiah 2:1-8)

454 BC

Appendix 6 – Watching for Jesus

"So Christ was once offered to bear the sins of many;
and unto them that look for him shall he appear the
second time *without sin unto salvation"* (Hebrews 9:28).

The Word of God says that Jesus is returning the second time to those who are looking for Him to return. Are you looking for Jesus to come again? If not, now is the time to start your watch because it is much later than most people think.

We do not know for certain the exact time that Jesus will return. Just before Jesus left this earth the first time, he told His disciples that He was going to return and He commanded them to *"watch."* What does it mean to continue watching?

Some of the things *"watching"* entails include:

1) Being aware of the prophetic signs in God's Word.
2) Living a life of holiness before our Lord.
3) Living a life separated from the world.
4) Encouraging one another with the wonderful Hope of His soon return.
5) Telling others Jesus is coming soon and of their need to be ready.
6) Praying the prayer Jesus taught us to pray in Luke 21:

*"And take heed to yourselves, lest at any time your hearts be overcharged with surfeiting, and drunkenness, and cares of this life, and so that day come upon you unawares. For like a snare shall it come on all them that dwell on the face of the whole earth. **Watch ye, therefore, and pray always, that ye may be accounted worthy to escape all these things that shall come to pass, and to stand before the Son of Man."***
(Luke 21:34-36 – KJ)

The act of *"watching"* is serious business with our Lord. If we fail to continue our diligence, Revelation 3:3 gives us fair warning:

> *"Remember therefore how thou hast received and heard, and hold fast, and repent. If therefore **thou shalt not watch**, I will **come on thee as a thief**, and thou **shalt not know** what hour I will come upon thee."*
> (Rev 3:3 – KJ)

Those who are not *"watching"* will be taken by surprise since a thief comes unannounced. The wise and faithful followers of Jesus; however, will continue *"watching"* for Him and they will not be surprised. Begin *"watching"* today before it is too late! Jesus is coming, very, very soon!

Are you ready if Jesus returned today? If you are not sure, please consider making the following prayer right now:

> *"Dear God in Heaven, I realize that I have not really been living my life for you. I humbly turn to you right now and ask you to forgive me. Dear Jesus, please rule and reign in my heart and life. Please help me to live for you for whatever time remains. I pray that I may be ready and that I may be able to stand before you when you return for me. In Jesus' name I pray. Amen."*

Our prayer is that many in the Church will pray this prayer and ask the Lord to help them be prepared for His return. We do not know for certain when Jesus will return, so we need to be ready every single day as we eagerly await His coming for us.

The words from Matthew Henry's commentary are also very good advice for the wise: "Therefore every day and every hour we must be ready, and not off our watch any day in the year, or any hour in the day" (M. H. Volume 5, Page 372).

Appendix 7 – Signs of Christ's Coming

As described earlier in this book, modern Bible teachers and students believe that the rebirth of the nation of Israel represents the budding of the *fig tree* that Jesus described to His disciples as he sat on the Mount of Olives, and we are living in the generation that won't pass away before He returns.

> *"Verily I say unto you, this generation shall not pass,*
> *till all these things be fulfilled"* (Mat 24:34 – KJ).

With Israel becoming a nation in 1948, we have been alerted that the Lord's return is fast approaching. Jesus also told his disciples a second sign to look for in the parable of Noah:

> *"As it was in the days of Noah,*
> *so it will be at the coming of the Son of Man."*
> (Mat 24:37 – NIV)

Here the Lord is telling the Church that just prior to his return, things will be the same as they were back in Noah's day. This pictures life going on right up until the day that the rapture occurs, and the judgments of God are suddenly released upon the earth. A careful study of Genesis 6 will alert the reader to the fact that living in these end times is almost parallel to the time before the flood. The world has become a great cesspool of corruption, violence, sex, drugs, idolatry, witchcraft and other perversions. Reading the account in Genesis is like reading today's newspaper or listening to the daily news.

In the Lord's parable concerning Noah, Jesus was also giving us a second important sign that His return is drawing very near. Several years ago a famous comet passed though our solar system and it was hailed at the most watched comet of all times.

Sign of Christ's Coming

April 8, 1997

Comet Hale-Bopp Over New York City
Credit and Copyright: J. Sivo
http://antwrp.gsfc.nasa.gov/apod/ap970408.html

"What's that point of light above the World Trade Center? It's Comet Hale-Bopp! Both faster than a speeding bullet and able to "leap" tall buildings in its single orbit, Comet Hale-Bopp is also bright enough to be seen even over the glowing lights of one of the world's premier cities. In the foreground lies the East River, while much of New York City's Lower Manhattan can be seen between the river and the comet."

> *"But as the days of Noe were, so shall also the coming*
> *of the Son of man be. For as in the days that were before*
> *the flood they were eating and drinking, marrying and*
> *giving in marriage, until the day that Noe entered into*
> *the ark, And knew not until the flood came, and took*
> *them all away; so shall also the coming of the Son of man be."*
> (Mat 24:37-39)

These words from our wonderful Lord have several applications about the generation that is about to witness the Lord's return.

Seas Lifted Up
Throughout the Old Testament, the time of the coming Tribulation period is described as the time when the "seas have lifted up," and also as coming in as a "flood" (please see Jeremiah 51:42, Hosea 5:10, Daniel 11:40 and Psalm 93:3-4 for just a few examples).

This is a direct parallel to the time of Noah when the Great Flood of water came to wipe out every living creature, except for righteous Noah and his family, and the pairs of animals that God spared. While God said that He would never flood the earth again with water, the coming Judgement will be by fire (see II Peter 3:10). The book of Revelation shows that billions of people are about to perish in the terrible time that lies just ahead (see Revelation 6:8 and 9:15).

2 Witnesses
A guiding principle of God is to establish a matter based upon the witness of two or more:

> "...a matter must be established by the testimony of two or three witnesses" (Deuteronomy 19:15 – NIV).

In 1994, God was able to get the attention of mankind when Comet Shoemaker-Levy crashed into Jupiter on the 9th of Av (on the Jewish calendar). Interestingly, this Comet was named after the "two" witnesses who first discovered it.

In 1995, "two" more astronomers also discovered another comet. It was called Comet Hale-Bopp and it reached its closest approach to planet Earth on March 23, 1997. It has been labeled as the most widely viewed comet in the history of mankind.

Scientists have determined that Comet Hale-Bopp's orbit brought it to our solar system 4,465 years ago (see Notes 1 and 2 below). In other words, the comet made its appearance near Earth in 1997 and also in 2468 BC. Remarkably, this comet preceded the Great Flood by 120 years! God warned Noah of this in Genesis 6:3:

> *"My Spirit shall not strive with man forever, for he is indeed flesh; yet his days shall be one hundred and twenty years."*

Days of Noah
What does all of this have to do with the Lord's return? Noah was born around 2948 BC, and Genesis 7:11, tells us that the Flood took place when Noah was 600, or in 2348 BC.

Remember, our Lord told us: ***"As it was in the days of Noah, so it will be at the coming of the Son of Man"*** (Matthew 24:37 – NIV).

In the original Greek, it is saying: ***"exactly like"*** it was, so it will be when He comes (see Strong's #5618).

During the days of Noah, Comet Hale-Bopp arrived on the scene as a harbinger of the Great Flood. Just as this same comet appeared before the Flood, could its arrival again in 1997 be a sign that God's final Judgement, also known as the time of great tribulation, is about to begin?

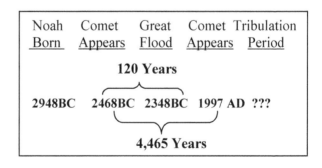

Comet Hale-Bopp arrived 120 years before the Flood as a warning to mankind. Only righteous Noah heeded God's warning and built the ark, as God instructed. By faith, Noah was obedient to God and, as a result, saved himself and his family from destruction.

Remember, Jesus told us His return would be preceded by great heavenly signs: *"And there shall be signs in the sun, and in the moon, and in the stars; and upon the earth distress of nations, with perplexity; the sea and the waves roaring..."* (Luke 21:25)

Just as this large comet appeared as a 120-year warning to Noah, its arrival in 1997 tells us that Jesus is getting ready to return again. Is this the **"Sign"** Jesus referred to?

Jesus was asked 3 questions by the disciples:
"Tell us, (1) when shall these things be" (the destruction of the city of Jerusalem), *"and (2) what shall be the __sign__ of thy coming, and (3) of the end of the world?"* (Matthew 24:3)

Sign of Christ's Coming

The **first** question had to do with events that were fulfilled in 70 AD. The **third** question has to do with the future time at the very end of the age.

The **second** question; however, has to do with the time of Christ's second coming. Jesus answered this second question in His description of the days of Noah found in Matthew 24:33-39:

> *(33) "So likewise ye, when ye shall see all these things, know that it is near, even at the doors. (34) Verily I say unto you, This generation shall not pass, till all these things be fulfilled. (35) Heaven and earth shall pass away, but my words shall not pass away. (36) But of that day and hour knoweth no man, no, not the angels of heaven, but my Father only. (37)* **But as the days of Noe were, so shall also the coming of the Son**

of man be. ⁽³⁸⁾*For as in the days that were before the flood they were eating and drinking, marrying and giving in marriage, until the day that Noe entered into the ark,* ⁽³⁹⁾ *And knew not until the flood came, and took them all away; so shall also the coming of the Son of man be."*

Jesus is telling us that the **sign** of His coming will be as it was during the days of Noah. As Comet Hale-Bopp was a sign to the people in Noah's day, its arrival in 1997 may be a sign that Jesus is coming back again soon. Comet Hale-Bopp could be the <u>very</u> <u>sign</u> Jesus was referring to, which would announce His return for His faithful.

Remember, Jesus said, *"exactly as it was in the days of Noah, so will it be when He returns."* The appearance of Comet Hale-Bopp in 1997 is a strong indication that the tribulation period is about to begin, but before then, Jesus is coming for His bride!

Keep looking up! Jesus is coming again very soon!
As Noah prepared for the destruction God warned him approximately 120 years before the Flood, Jesus has given mankind final warnings that we are living in the generation that will witness His return. We do not know how long a generation may be. For this reason we need to be wise like Noah and prepare by always remembering our Lord's instructions:

Watch and Pray
"(34) And take heed to yourselves, lest at any time your hearts be overcharged with surfeiting, and drunkenness, and cares of this life, and so that day come upon you unawares. (35) For as a snare shall it come on all them that dwell on the face of the whole earth. (36) **Watch ye therefore, and pray always, that ye may be accounted worthy to escape all these things that shall come to pass, and to stand before the Son of man"** (Luke 21:34-36).

(1) The original orbit of Comet Hale-Bopp was calculated to be approximately 265 years by engineer George Sanctuary in his article, ***Three Craters In Israel***, published on 3/31/01 found at: http://www.gsanctuary.com/3craters.html#3c_r13

Comet Hale-Bopp's orbit around the time of the Flood changed from 265 years to about 4,200 years. Because the plane of the comet's orbit is perpendicular to the earth's orbital plane (ecliptic), Mr. Sanctuary noted: "A negative time increment was used for this simulation…to back the comet away from the earth…. past Jupiter… and then out of the solar system. The simulation suggests that the past-past orbit had a very eccentric orbit with a period of only 265 years. When the comet passed Jupiter (***around 2203BC)*** its orbit was deflected upward, coming down near the earth 15 months later with the comet's period changed from 265 years to about (***4,200)*** years." (***added text*** *for clarity*)

(2) Don Yeomans, with NASA's Jet Propulsion Laboratory, made the following observations regarding the comet's orbit: "By integrating the above orbit forward and backward in time until the comet leaves the planetary system and then referring the osculating orbital elements…the following orbital periods result:

Original orbital period before entering planetary system = 4200 years. Future orbital period after exiting the planetary system = 2380 years."

This analysis can be found at:

http://www2.jpl.nasa.gov/comet/ephemjpl6.html

Based upon the above two calculations we have the following:

265 [a] + 4,200 [b] = 4,465 Years

1997 AD – 4,465 Years = 2468 BC = Hale Bopp arrived

(a) Orbit period calculated by George Sanctuary before deflection around 2203 BC.

(b) Orbit period calculated by Don Yeomans after 1997 visit.

Possible Updates

The primary focus of this book has been to discover the meaning of the visions given to Daniel. As these prophecies unfold in the events during these end times, we hope to update our website with **Supplemental Articles** that will help you prepare for the days ahead. Jesus is returning very, very soon. Our purpose is help you get ready.

Is God a Date Setter?

- God set a date for the flood and revealed it to righteous Noah (Gen 7:11).
- God set a date for the destruction of Sodom and revealed it to Abraham and Lot (Gen 18, 19).
- God set a date for Isaac to be born and told it to Sarah and Abraham (Gen 17:21).
- God set a date for Israel to come out of Egypt and revealed it centuries before he instructed Moses to do so (Gen 15:13; Gal 3:14-17; Exd 12:40).
- God set a date for the cattle of Egypt to die and told Moses and Pharaoh (Exd 12:40).
- God set a date for the defeat of Moab and revealed it to Isaiah earlier (Isa 16:14).
- God set a date for the end of the Babylonian captivity and revealed it to Jeremiah decades in advance (Jer 25:11).
- God set a date for the fall of Babylon and told it to Jeremiah and revealed it to Daniel (Jer 27:4-7; Dan 5:25-30).
- God set a date for the first coming of Jesus Christ and told it to Daniel, Mary, Joseph, and Simeon in advance (Dan 9; Mat 1:18-25; Luk 2:26-32).

"Surely the Lord God does nothing, unless He reveals His secret to His servants the prophets."
(Amo 3:7)

*"When the Spirit of truth comes, he will guide you into all the truth, for he will not speak on his own authority, but whatever he hears he will speak, and he will declare to you **the things that are to come**."*
(Jhn 16:16 – ESV)

Special Invitation

We hope that this book helps you see how very little time may remain and the need to know and love Jesus Christ before it's too late. If you have never been saved before, would you like to be saved? The Bible shows that it's simple to be saved...

- **Realize you are a sinner.**
  "As it is written, There is none righteous, no, not one:"
  (Romans 3:10)
  "... for there is no difference. For all have sinned, and come short of the glory of God;" (Romans 3:22-23)
- **Realize you CAN NOT save yourself.**
  "But we are all as an unclean thing, and all our righteousness are as filthy rags; ..." (Isaiah 64:6)
  "Not by works of righteousness which we have done, but according to his mercy he saved us, ..." (Titus 3:5)
- **Realize that Jesus Christ died on the cross to pay for your sins.**
  "Who his own self bare our sins in his own body on the tree,..." (I Peter 2:24)
  "... Unto him that loved us, and washed us from our sins in his own blood," (Revelation 1:5)
- **Simply by faith receive Jesus Christ as your personal Savior.**
  "But as many as received him, to them gave he power to become the sons of God, even to them that believe on his name:" (John 1:12)
  " ...Sirs, what must I do to be saved? And they said, Believe on the Lord Jesus Christ, and thou shalt be saved, and thy house." (Acts 16:30-31)
  "...if you confess with your mouth, 'Jesus is Lord,' and believe in your heart God raised him from the dead, you will be saved." (Romans 10:9 – NIV)

WOULD YOU LIKE TO BE SAVED?

If you would like to be saved, believe on the Lord Jesus Christ (Acts 16:31) right now by making the following confession of faith:

> Lord Jesus, I know that I am a sinner, and unless you save me, I am lost. I thank you for dying for me at Calvary. By faith I come to you now, Lord, the best way I know how, and ask you to save me. I believe that God raised you from the dead and acknowledge you as my personal Saviour.

If you believed on the Lord, this is the most important decision of your life. You are now saved by the precious blood of Jesus Christ, which was shed for you and your sins. Now that you have believed on Jesus as your personal Saviour, you will want to find a Church where you can be baptized as your first act of obedience, and where the Word of God is taught so you can continue to grow in your faith. Ask the Holy Spirit to help you as you read the Bible to learn all that God has for your life.

Also, see the Reference Notes and Bibliography section of this book, where you will find recommended books and websites that will help you on your wonderful journey.

Endtimes
The Bible indicates that we are living in the final days and Jesus Christ is getting ready to return very soon. This book was written to help people prepare to meet the Lord when He comes. The Word of God indicates that the tribulation period is rapidly approaching and that the Antichrist is getting ready to emerge on the world scene.

Jesus promised His disciples that there is a way to escape the horrible time of testing and persecution that will soon devastate this planet. One of the purposes of this book is to help you get prepared so you will be ready when Jesus Christ returns. We also highly recommend reading *Calling All Overcomers*, which covers the important book of Revelation.

About The Author

Jim Harman has been a Christian for 40 years. He has diligently studied the Word of God with a particular emphasis on Prophecy. Jim has written several books and the most essential titles are available at www.ProphecyCountdown.com: *Coming Spiritual Earthquake, The Kingdom, Overcomers' Guide To The Kingdom, Calling All Overcomers, Come Away My Beloved.* All of these books may be freely downloaded as PDF files and they will encourage you to continue *"Looking"* for the blessed hope of the Lord's soon return.

Jim's professional experience included being a Certified Public Accountant (CPA) and a Certified Property Manager (CPM). He had an extensive background in both public accounting and financial management with several well-known national firms.

Jim has been fortunate to have been acquainted with several mature believers who understand and teach the deeper truths of the Bible. It is Jim's strong desire that many will come to realize the importance of seeking the Kingdom and seeking Christ's righteousness as we approach the soon return of our Lord and Saviour Jesus Christ.

The burden of his heart is to see many come to know the joy of Christ's triumph in their life as they become true overcomers; qualified and ready to rule and reign with Christ in the coming Kingdom.

To contact the author for questions, to arrange for speaking engagements or to order multiple copies of this book:

Jim Harman
P.O. Box 941612
Maitland, FL 32794
JamesTHarman@aol.com

Excerpt from THE COMING SPIRITUAL EARTHQUAKE

An overcomer is a believer who has had an authentic experience with God. Though thrown into the furnace of affliction, they have come forth as pure gold. The overcomer is born through the victory they receive by trusting in Jesus Christ. Learning to be an overcomer is perhaps the most difficult thing to do on this earth as a human being. Possessing impressive credentials and degrees offer little solace when it comes to where the "rubber meets the road." Every professing Christian must learn to be an overcomer through faith and total trust in their Savior. In Matthew 11:28-30, Jesus urges: *"Come unto me, all ye that labour and are heavy laden, and I will give you rest. Take my yoke upon you, and learn of me; for I am meek and lowly in heart: and ye shall find rest unto your souls. For my yoke is easy, and my burden is light."* The overcomers take their agony and burdens to the mighty counselor. Through prayer and trust, Jesus leads the downcast believer to "green pasture." The sting of the adversary is somehow turned to sweet victory. Christ alone is able to provide the peace that passes all understanding. While every believer will have trials and testing in this world, Christ reminded us to be of good cheer because He overcame this world. As believers, we find our sweet victory in Him! Overcomers are believers who find their strength and help in Him--not through man, but by the power of the Son of God. A genuine overcomer follows in Christ's footsteps. They learn to "take it on the chin" and to "take it to the cross." Whatever the world dishes out is handled with prayer and placed on the altar before God. By offering everything to Christ, they find hope and sufficiency in Him. Being an overcomer is what being a Christian is all about. Through the trials of this life, the overcomers' faith is put on trial and thereby confirmed as Holy evidence before a mighty God, it is authentic. As our example, Jesus endured the cross for the joy set before Him. Overcomers have the victory because of His victory. Through His victory, the overcomer is able to walk in newness of life. The overcomer knows: they have been crucified with Christ and their old life is gone (Gal 2:20). By dying to self, the overcomer experiences the joy of Christ's triumph in their life. Finally, an overcomer is grateful and humble: for they know of God's rich mercy and marvelous grace. If it wasn't for Christ, they would be doomed. Out of this gratitude, rises the song of gladness and praise. An overcomers' heart bursts forth with praise and adoration unto their God for the victory He provides. The overcomer knows, first hand, that while weeping may endure for the night: joy cometh in the morning!

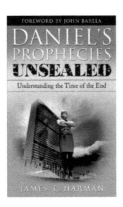

"Go your way Daniel, because the words are closed up and sealed until the time of the end...none of the wicked will understand, but those who are wise will understand."
(Daniel 12:9-10)

The Archangel Michael told Daniel that the prophecies would be sealed until the time of the end. Discover how the prophecies in the book of Daniel are being unsealed in the events taking place today.

Since Daniel was told that the wise will understand the message and lead many to righteousness, while the wicked will not grasp its meaning and will continue in their wickedness, it is imperative for everyone living in these end times to diligently examine and attempt to comprehend the vital message Daniel has recorded for us. The wise will diligently search the word of the Lord and ask for wisdom in order to understand God's plan.

When Jesus came the first time, the wise men of the day were aware of His soon arrival and they were actively looking for Him. Today, those who are wise will be passionately sharing this message and helping others prepare. Those doing so will *"shine like the stars forever and ever."*

May the Lord grant us a heart of wisdom to understand the time we are living in so we can prepare for what lies ahead!

Download your FREE copy: www.ProphecyCountdown.com

Or from Amazon.com – Available in Paperback and or Kindle Edition

An Interpretation of the Song of Solomon
Foreword by John Zajac
James T. Harman

God placed the Song of Solomon in the heart of the Bible for a special reason. ***Come Away My Beloved*** helps reveal that reason in a most enchanting way. In this refreshing commentary you will realize why this ancient love story has perplexed Bible students and commentators down through the ages.

Find out the prophetic importance veiled within the Song's poetic imagery and experience a renewed love for the Lord as you explore one of the most passionate love stories of all time.

Witness the wonderful joys of romance and devotion shared by two young lovers. Discover enduring lessons of virtue and faithfulness, and learn amazing truths that have been hidden within the greatest love Song ever written.

Written almost 3,000 years ago this brilliant Song of love reflects God's desire for every man and woman; not only in their present lives but also in their relationship with Him.

This book will revive your heart with a fervent love for your Saviour. It will also help you prepare for your glorious wedding day when Jesus returns for His devoted bride.

Allow this beautiful story of love and passion to ignite a flame in your heart and let this inspirational Song arouse your heart to join in the impassioned cry with the rest of the bride:

"Make haste, my beloved, and come quickly…"

Download your FREE copy: www.ProphecyCountdown.com

Or from Amazon.com – Available in Paperback and or Kindle Edition

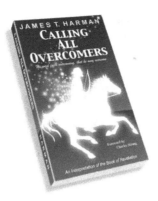

Perplexed by the book of Revelation? Not sure what all the signs, symbols and metaphors really mean? Jim Harman's latest work unravels Apostle John's remarkable revelation of Jesus Christ and what's in store for the inhabitants of planet Earth. This extraordinary commentary is not another cookie-cutter rehash of the popular teachings fostered by the *Left Behind* phenomena so prevalent in today's church.

One of the central messages in the book of Revelation is that God is calling men to be genuine overcomers. Jesus Christ has been sent out from the throne of God to conquer men's hearts so they can also be overcomers.

The purpose of this book is to encourage people to embrace him as the King of their heart and allow his life to reign in theirs. He wants you to be able to overcome by his mighty power and strength living inside of you just as He overcame for all of us. Jesus will be looking for a faithful remnant qualified to rule and reign with him when he returns. This book will help you prepare to be the overcomer Jesus will be looking for.

The reader will come away with a new and enlightened understanding of what the last book in God's Word is all about. Understand the book of Revelation and why it is so important for believers living in the last days of the Church age.

Download your FREE copy: www.ProphecyCountdown.com

Or from Amazon.com – Available in Paperback and or Kindle Edition

Once a person is saved, the number one priority should be seeking entrance into the Kingdom through the salvation of their soul. It is pictured as a runner in a race seeking a prize represented by a crown that will last forever.

The salvation of the soul and entrance into the coming Kingdom are only achieved through much testing and the trial of one's faith. If you are going through difficulty, then REJOICE:

> *"Blessed is the man who perseveres under trial, because when he has stood the test, he will receive the crown of life that God has promised to those who love Him."* (James 1:12)

The "Traditional" teaching on the "THE KINGDOM" has taken the Church captive into believing all Christians will rule and reign with Christ no matter if they have lived faithful and obedient lives, or if they have been slothful and disobedient with the talents God has given them. Find out the important Truth before Jesus Christ returns.

MUST READING FOR EVERY CHRISTIAN

Jesus Christ is returning for His faithful overcoming followers. Don't miss the opportunity of ruling and reigning with Christ in the coming KINGDOM!

Download your FREE copy: www.ProphecyCountdown.com

Or from Amazon.com – Available in Paperback and or Kindle Edition

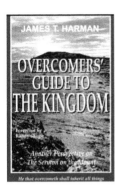

Get ready to climb back up the Mountain to listen to Christ's teachings once again. Though you may have read this great Sermon on the Mount many times, discover exciting promises that many have missed.

The purpose of this book is to help Christians be the Overcomers that Jesus wants them to be and to help them gain their own entrance in the coming Kingdom. Learn what seeking the Kingdom of God is all about and be among the chosen few who will "enter into" the coming Kingdom. *"Whoever hears these sayings of Mine, and does them, I will liken him to a wise man who built his house upon the rock."* (Mat 7:24)

Also learn about:
- The link between Beatitudes and Fruit of the Spirit
- What the "law of Christ" really is
- The critical importance of the "Lord's prayer"
- How to be an Overcomer
- THE SIGN of Christ's soon Coming
- A new song entitled: LOOKING FOR THE SON which has the message of how vitally important it is to be Watching for the Lord's return and the consequences to those who are not looking.

Download your FREE copy: www.ProphecyCountdown.com

Or from Amazon.com – Available in Paperback and or Kindle Edition

LOOKING FOR THE SON
Lyrics by Jim Harman
Can be sung to the hit tune: *"ROLLING IN THE DEEP"*

Lyric	Scripture
There's a fire burning in my heart	Luke 24:32
Yearning for the Lord to come,	Rev. 22:17, Mat. 6:33
and His Kingdom come to start	
Soon He'll come.....so enter the narrow gate	Lk. 21:34-36,Mat.7:13
Even though you mock me now...	II Peter 3:4
He'll come to set things straight	
Watch how I'll leave in the twinkling of an eye	I Corinthians 15:52
Don't be surprised when I go up in the sky	Revelation 3:10
There's a fire burning in my heart	Luke 24:32
Yearning for my precious Lord	Revelation 22:17
And His Kingdom come to start	Revelation 20:4-6
Your love of this world, has forsaken His	I John 2:15
It leaves me knowing that you could have had it all	Revelation 21:7
Your love of this world, was oh so reckless	Revelation 3:14-22
I can't help thinking	Philippians 1:3-6
You would have had it all	Revelation 21:7
Looking for the Son	Titus 2:13, Luke 21:36
(Tears are gonna fall, not looking for the Son)	Matthew 25:10-13
You had His holy Word in your hand	II Timothy 3:16
(You're gonna wish you had listened to me)	Jeremiah 25:4-8
And you missed it...for your self	Matthew 22:11-14
(Tears are gonna fall, not looking for the Son)	Matthew 25:10-13
Brother, I have a story to be told	Habakkuk 2:2
It's the only one that's true	John 3:16-17
And it should've made your heart turn	II Peter 3:9
Remember me when I rise up in the air	I Corinthians 15:52
Leaving your home down here	I Corinthians 15:52
For true Treasures beyond compare	Matthew 6:20
Your love of this world, has forsaken His	I John 2:15
It leaves me knowing that you could have had it all	Revelation 21:7
Your love of this world, was oh so reckless	Revelation 3:14-22
I can't help thinking	Philippians 1:3-6
You would have had it all	Revelation 21:7

(Lyrics in parentheses represent background vocals)
(CONTINUED)

Lyric	Scripture
Looking for the Son	Titus 2:13, Lk. 21:36
(Tears are gonna fall, not looking for the Son)	Matthew 25:10-13
You had His holy Word in your hand	II Timothy 3:16
(You're gonna wish you had listened to me)	Jeremiah 25:4-8
And you lost it...for your self	Matthew 22:11-14
(Tears are gonna fall, not looking for the Son)	Matthew 25:10-13
You would have had it all	Revelation 21:7
Looking for the Son	Titus 2:13, Lk. 21:36
You had His holy Word in your hand	II Timothy 3:16
But you missed it... for your self	Matthew 22:11-14

Lyric	Scripture
Lov'n the world....not the open door	I Jn. 2:15, Rev. 4:1
Down the broad way... blind to what life's really for	Matthew 7:13-14
Turn around now...while there still is time	I Jn. 1:9, II Pet. 3:9
Learn your lesson now or you'll reap just what you sow	Galatians 6:7

(You're gonna wish you had listened to me)
You would have had it all
(Tears are gonna fall, not looking for the Son)
You would have had it all
(You're gonna wish you had listened to me)
It all, it all, it all
(Tears are gonna fall, not looking for the Son)

You would have had it all
(You're gonna wish you had listened to me)
Looking for the Son
(Tears are gonna fall, not looking for the Son)
You had His holy Word in your hand
(You're gonna wish you had listened to me)
And you missed it...for your self
(Tears are gonna fall, not looking for the Son)

You would have had it all
(You're gonna wish you had listened to me)
Looking for the Son
(Tears are gonna fall, not looking for the Son)
You had His holy Word in your hand
(You're gonna wish you had listened to me)
But you missed it
You missed it
You missed it
You missed it....for your self

Scripture Summary
Jeremiah 25:4-8
Habakkuk 2:2
Matthew 6:20
Matthew 6:33
Matthew 7:13
Matthew 22:11-14
Matthew 25:10-13
Luke 21:34-36
Luke 24:332
John 3:16-17
I Corinthians 15:52
Galatians 6:7
Philippians 1:3-6
II Timothy 3:16
Titus 2:13
II Peter 3:9
II Peter 3:4
I John 1:9
I John 2:15
Revelation 3:10
Revelation 3:14-22
Revelation 4:1
Revelation 20:4-6
Revelation 21:7
Revelation 22:17

(See www.ProphecyCountdown.com for more information)

The Day of the Lord is Near!

The Coming Spiritual Earthquake

by James T. Harman

"The Message presented in this book is greatly needed to awaken believers to the false ideas many have when it comes to the Rapture. I might have titled it: THE RAPTURE EARTHQUAKE!"
Ray Brubaker - God's News Behind the News

"If I am wrong, anyone who follows the directions given in this book will be better off spiritually. If I am right, they will be among the few to escape the greatest spiritual calamity of the ages."
Jim Harman - Author

**MUST READING FOR EVERY CHRISTIAN!
HURRY! BEFORE IT IS TOO LATE!**

CPSIA information can be obtained
at www.ICGtesting.com
Printed in the USA
BVHW060949300620
582506BV00006B/445